Mile by Mile on the Settle-Carlisle

STAINFORTH SIDINGS

Why was this line across the spine of England ever built? The answer is short and rude. . . to put the lordly London & North Western Railway in its place at Carlisle. For a short while this the Midland Railway achieved.

Derek Cross.

Now - £4

MILE BY MILE
ON THE
SETTLE-CARLISLE

W R MITCHELL

ILLUSTRATED BY PETER FOX

FOREWORD BY MIKE HARDING

RIBBLEHEAD VIADUCT

CASTLEBERG
1997

To
The Doctors and Staff of the Fracture Clinic and Occupational Therapy department of Airedale General Hospital without whom I could not have typed this book.

GARSDALE TANK HOUSE

A **Castleberg** Book.

First published in the United Kingdom in 1997.

ISBN 1 871064 74 0

Typeset in Palacio, printed and bound in the United Kingdom by Lamberts Printers, Station Road, Settle, North Yorkshire, BD24 9AA.

Published by Castleberg, 18 Yealand Avenue, Giggleswick, Settle, North Yorkshire, BD24 0AY.

Contents

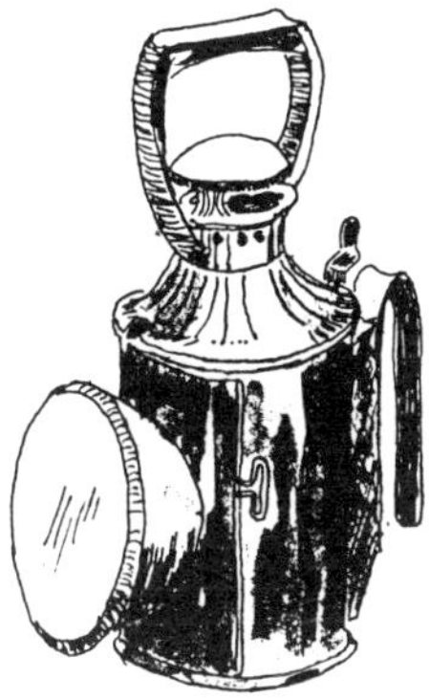

Illustrations

All the illustrations — cover pictures, photographs, line drawings and maps — were provided by Peter Fox.

Mile by Mile

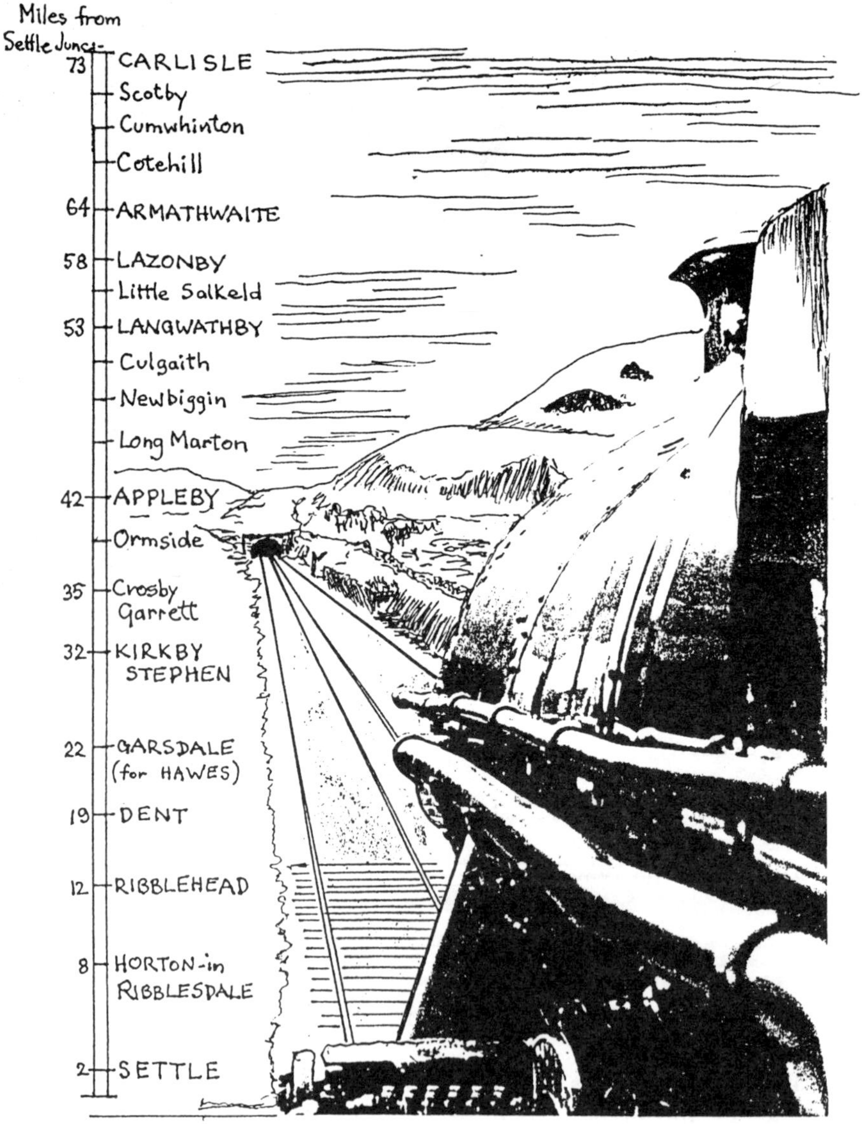
Miles from
Settle Junct.
73 CARLISLE
Scotby
Cumwhinton
Cotehill
64 ARMATHWAITE
58 LAZONBY
Little Salkeld
53 LANGWATHBY
Culgaith
Newbiggin
Long Marton
42 APPLEBY
Ormside
35 Crosby Garrett
32 KIRKBY STEPHEN
22 GARSDALE (for HAWES)
19 DENT
12 RIBBLEHEAD
8 HORTON-in RIBBLESDALE
2 SETTLE

Foreword

by
Mike Harding

WHEN I first came to the Dales as a kid on a push bike, cycling through the ghost town of Burnley (it was Wakes Week) and climbing by Nelson over Gisburn to Long Preston, I found myself, for the last part of the journey, following the Settle-Carlisle line, along by the Ribble towards Settle.

On that hot summer's afternoon, as my tired legs took me alongside the line by butterbur and campion, a Black Five came snorting down from Settle belching steam and smoke, roaring past like a great iron monster.

Years later I came to live in the Dales, in a former railwayman's cottage right by the line. Night mails from Scotland rushed past the gable end, goods heading north trundled up the long drag, 'steam specials' like the Nigel Gresley had us all out with our cameras.

I came to be fascinated by the line. Like the Ancient Mariner, I would stop one in three and regale them with details and facts until they grew glassy-eyed and quoted the *habeus corpus* act at me.

It is a truly fascinating line, every inch, every nut and bolt with a story to tell.

No better man for telling the story may be be found than Bill Mitchell, who must know more about the line than anybody. As a guide to what you see as the line passes the carriage window, you couldn't pick a better man or book.

INAUGURATION OF THE PASSENGER SERVICE

Introduction

> Unlike many routes, it was designed as a whole, and possesses a remarkable unity of design from one end to the other in both structural and architectural terms.
> *National Railway Museum.*

THE Settle-Carlisle railway provides an introduction to the Northern Pennines, comprising some of the finest upland landscape in England. Carriage windows frame scenery on a grand scale. There is variety between tracts of bleak moorland, where tough horned sheep graze, and the u-shaped valleys known as dales, where farms are linked together by miles of drystone walls and life was satisfying but never easy.

Memorable moments on the Settle-Carlisle include a glimpse of flat-topped Ingleborough as the train crosses the 24 high arches of Ribblehead viaduct, and the sudden appearance of verdant Dentdale after the constriction of 2,629 yard long Blea Moor Tunnel, some 500 feet below a breezy moor which is divided between Yorkshire and Cumbria. From the Appleby district, the traveller sees a procession of Pennine hills—Defoe's 'wall of brass'—along the eastern skyline.

The Settle-Carlisle is a superb example of Victorian engineering—a no-nonsense, all-weather link with Scotland. The railway was intended to take expresses travelling at up to 90 miles an hour on a gradient not exceeding 1 in 100, with a comfortable crossing of the watershed at Aisgill, 1,169 feet above sea level, close to the sources of Ure and Eden. The response of Midland brass, brains and brawn to the need for their own rail link with Scotland was to devise a system which did not dodge difficulties. It was to include 325 bridges, 21 viaducts and 14 tunnels. The embankments, each absorbing around a quarter of a million cubic yards of material, were by themselves objects of wonderment to Victorian sightseers.

Every big project needs a hero. The man who deserves most credit for the Settle-Carlisle is John Crossley, resident engineer, who delayed his retirement to supervise the work and died not long after the line was opened in 1876. His railway, built hurriedly, almost frenziedly, in the 1870s, a time of bad weather, financial pressures and inflation, has a unity of design, being recognisably Midland from end to end. Only Culgaith station departs from the norm of 'Derby Gothic'.

The Settle-Carlisle sprang out of inter-company rivalry with the London and North Western and was primarily the Midland bid for a share in the lucrative Scottish traffic. Thus local traffic was of secondary importance. No attempt was made to link up every small village en route, nor indeed to take the easier option from Ribblehead of traversing Widdale to Hawes and from here to Garsdale.

The sites of some stations were decided on only after long periods of discussion and a selection from several choices. Dent station, the subject of several changes of location, was eventually constructed by the old 'coal road' to Garsdale and was over four miles distant and 600 ft higher than the village of Dent (grandly referred to by the natives as Dent Town). The structures of the Settle-Carlisle differ subtly according to the local building material, basically grey limestone in the south and new red sandstone in the north. After 120 years, the line has become a part of the landscape, accentuating the natural contours.

This is said to have been the last important railway in Britain to be built by the traditional pick and shovel method and the recruitment of thousands of navvies. Guesstimations of the size of the labour force are usually extreme (in fact, it peaked at around 6,000 for the whole route). Steam cranes lifted dressed stones on to the viaducts. Vertical steam engines were installed at the head of shafts and on the steep flanks of hills.

Fussy little contractors' engines hauled trucks on tramways, carrying coal, provisions and (on Saturday afternoons at Ribblehead) people. As the line was nearing completion, the Burleigh drill succeeded hand-drilling in various places and a new type of machine being tested included one capable of dealing with boulder-clay, a nightmare to engineers.

When I first studied the life and traditions of the Settle-Carlisle, the Steam Age was in its twilight period and diesel-hauled traffic was being seen. A fireman going on duty looked carefully to see which type of engine was arriving. He did not know in advance if he would be working with Steam or Diesel. In the former case, he would say: "It's a do-it-yourself. I'll have to shovel the coal today."

Black armbands were worn by sufferers from Settle-Carlitis when, on Saturday, August 11, 1968, steam traction came to an end. Anyone who travelled on the last steam train over the Settle-Carlisle was charged 15 guineas—and was delighted to have the opportunity to pay. Then, ten years later, steam was back in grand style as (on March 25, 1978), *Green Arrow* stormed the line with a charter train. It was the wrong colour for an old Midland route, but thousands who stood at the lineside, with rain or sleet in their faces, cheered as the train emerged from a Pennine mist.

Mile by Mile on the Settle-Carlisle is a companion guide to the famous railway, offering basic information on the main features such as stations, signalboxes, viaducts and tunnels. Supporting notes of a gossipy nature will add to your knowledge and enjoyment of the route. They deal mainly with operational matters rather than the oft-repeated details of the construction period.

Tribute is paid to the workers—footplate men, signalmen

(and women), plus their families—who took over when the line was built and kept it operational in all weathers. It has been a joy over the years to share their memories and, now and again, to enjoy the hospitality of a signal box, where strong tea was virtually on tap.

I have tasted food cooked on a footplate shovel and it was at Settle Junction, just before his retirement after long service, that Derek Soames introduced me to the delights of toasted kipper. He collected a toasting fork from a hook and sat on a stool within easy range of a chery-red fire. With experienced ease, Derek balanced the kipper on the fork and gently positioned it over the coals. Almost immediately, the kipper began to sizzle. The box was filled with an aroma so strong and attractive it must surely have made cats' noses twitch up to a mile away. Droplets of fat made the fire hiss. The head and tail of the kipper began to blaze. Derek transferred the kipper on to a warm plate and set about cooking the second fish. It was done in not much more than a minute.

The permanent way men tended to sit on the rails at 'snap' time. These workers were a 'scratch' lot, drawn from many areas. One gang of permanent way men became known as the Foreign Legion, "because there wasn't two of us belonged to t'same part of t'country." Collecting their stories was, for me, just as important as studying the official records of the railway, or making a technical study of the locomotives, the Steamers and their successors, the Sprinters, which drink diesel oil and are long and lean, like greyhounds.

The Terrain

> The chief aesthetic appeal is in the viaducts. . . and their setting in the wild open hill country of the Yorkshire Dales.
> *Countryside Commission.*

THE Settle-Carlisle is generally uplifted, offering wide views. An early exception is Langcliffe Cutting, just north of Settle. In this deep, dark, damp gorge, echoes pursue each other and in autumn proud trains slip and slither on fallen leaves which earlier traffic has squashed into pulp on the rails.

Scenically, the Settle-Carlisle may be divided into three sections. The most southern terrain is largely grey and green—the grey of limestone outcrops and a futuristic pattern of walls, the green being the verdant pastures, backed by the dun colours of moorland. Dominating the scene are three peaks—Whernside, Ingleborough and Penyghent—each attaining mountainhood by over-topping the 2,000 ft contour line. A photographer's viewpoint made famous by Treacy, the Railway Bishop, is just north of Horton-in-Ribblesdale, where rail traffic occupies an embankment and the backdrop includes the leonine form of Penyghent.

A second main type of scenery consists of upland dales and expansive moors between Ribblehead and Kirkby Stephen. The dales, chiselled out by glaciers, are served by narrow roads which have an aversion to going straight and may occasionally be unremittingly steep. The Settle-Carlisle takes a much easier course. Above Dentdale, the guard of a goods train on a ledge cut from the flanks of Knoutberry waved at the pilot of a low-flying Spitfire aircraft.

Thirdly, there is the Eden Valley, with outcropping sandstone with so red a hue it looks in places as though the landscape and the railway structures sprouting from it are having a bad attack of capillary bleeding.

It is a line for superlatives, boasting of the highest main line station in England (Dent) and what were, until removal, the highest water troughs in the world (Garsdale). Smardale viaduct is the highest on the line. At Ribblehead, a former playground of glaciers, as evidenced by low smooth hills called drumlins (containing glacial debris), a 440 yard long viaduct is the largest, most notable (and expensive) feature.

In the construction of Ribblehead viaduct, over 30,000 cubic yards of stone was transported here from Littledale, yet twenty-four lofty arches give it an appearance which belies its considerable weight. Blea Moor Tunnel, 2,629 yards long, has a diminutive seam of coal which has been hacked away by men wanting an unusual souvenir to show their family and friends—a fragment of coal from the Blea Moor pit!

The Eden Valley opens like a great fan between the north-south alignment of Pennine fells and the Lake District. For miles on end, the Settle-Carlisle is lost to users of the main roads. At Ormside and Eden Lacy, coffer dams had to be made for piers which had to stand in the river. At the Eden Gorge, landslips were frequent until the foundations of the new railway had bonded.

In 72 miles, the line loses itself in a mass of tracks at Carlisle, gateway to Scotland.

Pennine Weather

Stationmasters and signalmen between Hellifield and Carlisle must carefully watch the weather during the winter months.
The General Appendix.

TO BE honest, the Pennine weather is generally cloudy. Mist as damp as a dish-clout (cloth) clings to the valleys. The big hills are often bonneted by cloud. On a bad day, rain will trickle down the carriage window and visibility will be limited. On a good day—the views are sublime, especially in winter when, with the high fells under snow and ice, a laggard sun turns them from pink to gold.

A westerly gale, funnelled by the Lune Valley and Chapel-le-Dale, plays a tuba solo in the high arches of Ribblehead viaduct. In stormy weather, men used to gather to tighten the tarpaulin covers of goods wagons before a train was permitted to cross the viaduct. A high wind had a braking effect on cattle wagons and sometimes brought the whole train to a standstill at the approaches to the viaduct.

Men on duty at snowtime cleaned out points and attended to signals. When frosty nights were forecast in this exposed area, a stove was lit to keep the water-crane at Blea Moor operative. In time of fog, a man sat in a small cabin near the distant signal. When the signal was 'on' he put a detonator on the rail, removing it when the signal came off.

Ribblehead became a weather station in 1938. Records were kept of wind strength, rainfall and height of the cloud base. The latter was usually assessed in relation to the Three Peaks, but when there was doubt a balloon was released from the platform and its upward progress timed. Every hour of every day, from 7am until 9pm, the telephone rang in the Stationmaster's Office and coded details were given to a representative of the Air Ministry. A rain gauge, installed in 1954, had a first year total of 109½ inches. Five inches of rain were recorded on one day in December.

Dent, the highest station, was in everyone's mind when a north-east blizzard deposited snow which stuck. Snow drifted near Ribblehead and during the 1947 blockage, a jet engine obtained from Rolls Royce of Barnoldswick and placed on a flat wagon was confidentally expected to disperse the drifts. So hard was the snow packed that the experiment was called off when a mere 30 yards of snow had been cleared.

DENT HEAD VIADUCT

The weather-gods were at their most cruel during a stormy period in January, 1995, when sections of line were flooded and, above Mallerstang, a landslip blocked the down-line and derailed a passenger train. A train using the up-line could not be warned and a collision took place. Stuart Wilson, the conductor on the first passenger train, lost his life.

The Eden Valley has its own special wind, the Helm, which is created when air from the east, cooled during its ascent of the more gentle eastern slopes of the fells, suddenly plunges over the western rim to meet the warmer air of the vale. The turbulence rages along the East Fellside to around Garsdale and at its most savage has been known to blight the spring pastures and blow slates from the roofs of farms and cottages. It is also said to have blown coal from the shovels of firemen on the open-sided footplates of trains. The Helm Wind does not usually cross the Eden.

History and Folklore

...you sense that the people who live here have to be as hardy as the sheep which graze the drystone wall encompassed pastures.
Pearson's Railway Rides (1991).

THE VIEW from the carriage window, between Settle and Carlisle, takes in not only the grandeur of fells and waterfalls going white with fury as they descend near vertical slopes. There is more to be seen than the broad sweep of boat-shaped dales where glacial ice had gouged the rock and left a covering of mush we call 'boulder clay'.

Rather more subtle are the traces of early farming, where Man worked the light limestone soils. To the knowing eye, ridges and circlets in North Ribblesdale relate to hutments and field systems of the Bronze and Iron Ages. The free-draining limestone country made habitation possible when much of the area was wooded and the low ground either lake or marsh. At Ribblehead, the line crosses the course of a Roman road which, beginning at the fort at what is now Bainbridge in Wensleydale, has traversed Cam End ('the devil's highway') and descended to follow the old route through Chapel-le-Dale and on to Lunesdale.

For several centuries, what is now thought of as the Settle-Carlisle corridor was settled by immigrants from the Continent and Scandinavia who arrived from the east. In Edenvale and Ribblesdale, between the 7th and 9th centuries, first Angles, then Danes found tolerable conditions on the lower ground, where they were soon breaking out land with the plough. The basic settlement pattern of small villages and groups of small farms in Edenvale and Ribblesdale was established by new settlers.

The Norsefolk, who came in the 10th century, made the daleheads their own. They were descendants of Scandinavians whose migration route lay round the north of Scotland and the Western Isles to a landfall in Ireland (where many would marry red-haired native girls), thence across the Irish Sea to a landfall on the north-west coast of England and a penetration of the higher country which was still 'up for grabs'.

Norsefolk were pastoralists who abhored crowds. In the dale country they re-established something of the pattern their ancestors had known in Scandinavia. They had their winter houses in the dales and their *saeters,* or the summer grazing grounds, where their stock—cattle, sheep, goats—might take advantage of the summer flush of grass, leaving the home acres to grow grass to be harvested as hay. A Norse farm has been excavated at Ribblehead, at what is now the rim of the quarried area to the west of the railway station. Norse names for natural features include fell, dale, moss, beck, crag—all to be seen from the Settle-Carlisle.

In the 12th century, when the motto of Kendal was 'wool is my bread', Appleby was thriving as a borough which became the capital town of Westmorland, its main street dominated by a Castle which for centuries was one of a string of fortified places presided over by the Clifford family, originally de Punt, who were on the Welsh Marches before moving to those facing Scotland and had estates extending southwards into Craven. Pendragon, in Mallerstang, viewed by the railway traveller from a high elevation, was one of their castles.

The best-known member of the family, Lady Anne, was almost a Queen of the Dales. A great traveller by coach, she gloried in covering some of the rough upland routes, such as that leading to Hell Gill Bridge, not far from Aisgill, the highest point on the Settle-Carlisle line. Lady Anne took her favourite bed with her on her journeys between the Clifford lands of Craven and Westmorland.

Along the green lanes which may be seen from the train (an especially good one passes under an arch of Arten Gill viaduct) goods were moved by pack pony. These routes were also used for livestock, even flocks of geese for market, their webbed feet reinforced against the rough ground by tar, then sand, through which the birds were driven at the start of the trip.

For centuries, fleeces taken from the backs of the horned sheep was a major stimulus for trade. In medieval days, the big monasteries—including Fountains, Furness and Sawley—worshipped Mammon as well as God. A vast area of grazing land on the Pennines and in central Lakeland was used by Fountains, in Yorkshire, who had close links with Continental wool merchants. Wool distributed from Kendal to Dent and other villages in the upper Dales sustained a hand-knitting industry which augmented the income of dalesfolk at a time when farming was impoverished.

The pastures of Craven were renowned for stock-breeding. Cattle from Scotland, driven on the hoof, were sold at Gearstones, near Ribblehead, at Great Close on Malham Moor and other places, and after being fattened up went to the markets of the burgeoning English towns. The sale of cattle, which was casual, held in special venues or the main streets of towns on market days, was eventually formalised, trading taking place in auction marts. By this time, the railway was the principal transporter of stock into England.

The landscape viewed from the Settle-Carlisle has a tidiness derived from the Enclosures of the 18th and 19th centuries, when common land on which many had rights was parcelled up into plots owned by a few, who erected drystone walls and began to improve their farming methods, employing as labourers some of those who previously had equal rights with them. Notice, as the train goes through limestone areas, the many field kilns where limestone was burnt (using coal from thin seams in the Yoredale series of rocks) and either used domestically or spread about the land to sweeten it.

The field kilns have long been idle, their work taken over by the big quarries, such as that at Horton-in-Ribblesdale. Many hill farms have been amalgamated to form big units run by one or two people, so the rural areas have become depopulated, with a loss of local amenties such as schools. This is the Age of Leisure and Pleasure. The Settle-Carlisle is largely a tourist line, though encouragingly—in recent times—there has been an upsurge of freight traffic, principally gypsum for Kirkby Thore and coal en route for Scotland.

Some of the drollest stories of the Settle-Carlisle concern the days when railwaymen donned khaki in the evening and operated as the Home Guard. It is said that the stationmaster at Ribblehead mistook plumes of steam escaping from the ventilating shafts of Blea Moor on a cold autumn morning for German parachutists. Derek Cross, commenting on this tale, wrote: "God knows what the Germans would have made of Blea Moor, especially if one had fallen down a ventilating shaft!"

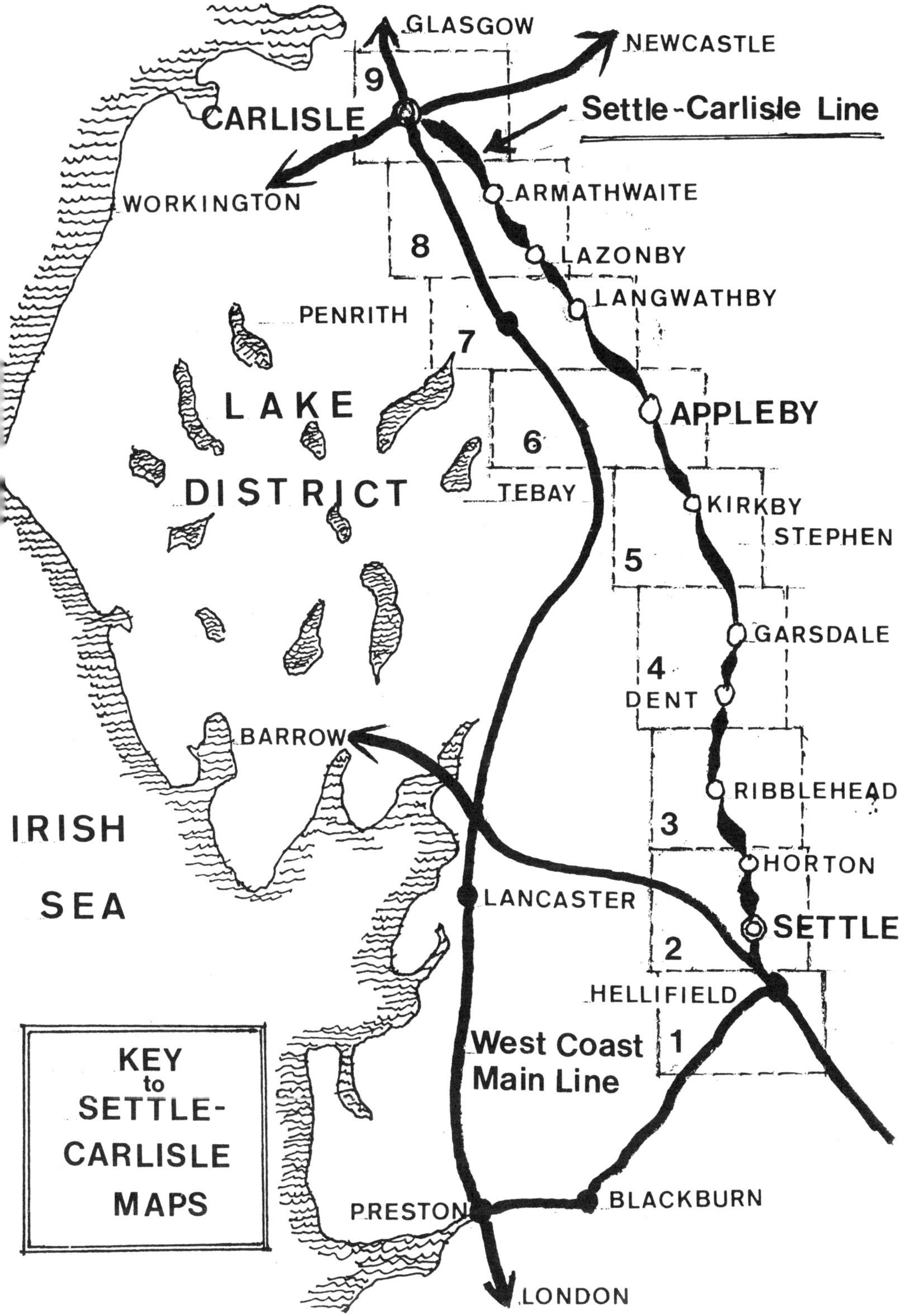

MAPS NOT TO SCALE

1000
M R
1000

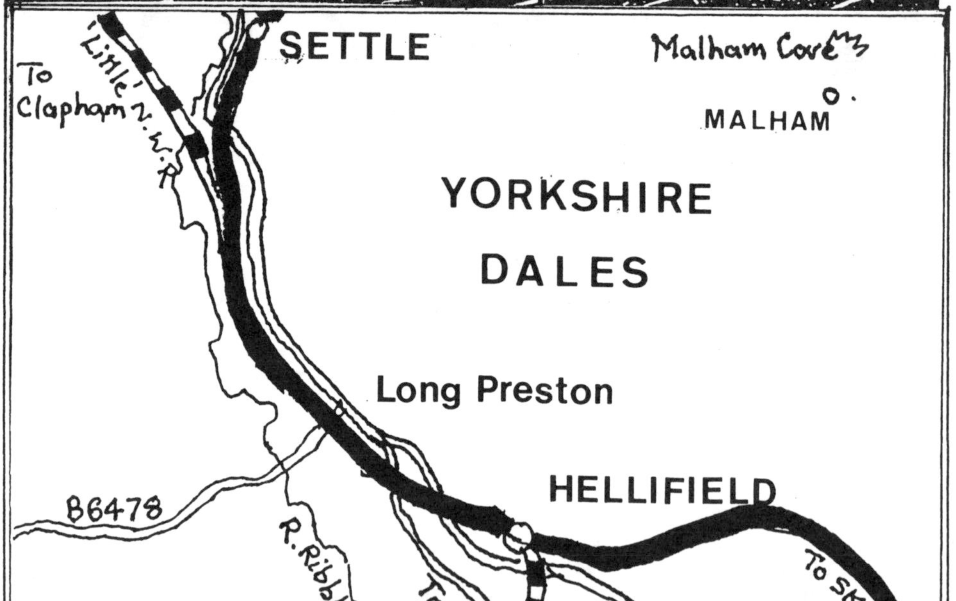
SETTLE
Malham Cove
MALHAM
To Clapham
'Little' N.W.R
YORKSHIRE
DALES
Long Preston
HELLIFIELD
B6478
R. Ribble
To Gisburn
A682
ex L&Y.R.
A65
To Leeds
To Skipton
1

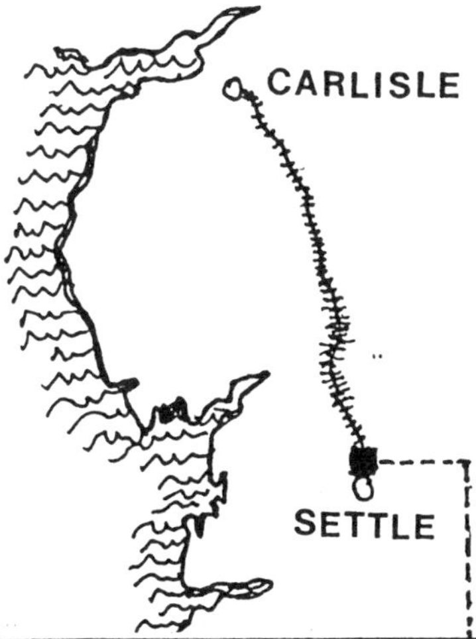
CARLISLE
SETTLE

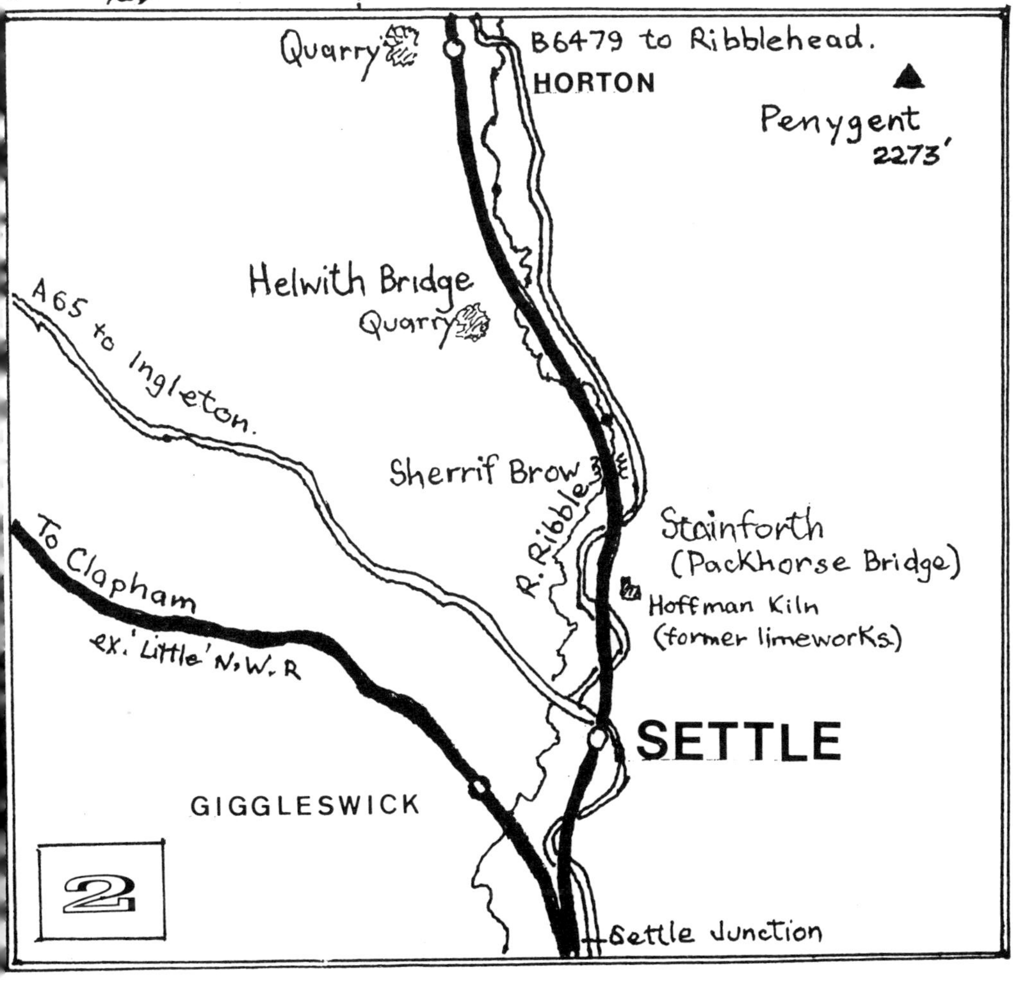
Quarry
B6479 to Ribblehead.
HORTON
Penygent
2273'
Helwith Bridge
Quarry
A65 to Ingleton.
Sherrif Brow
R. Ribble
Stainforth
(Packhorse Bridge)
Hoffman Kiln
(former limeworks)
To Clapham
ex. 'Little' N.W.R
SETTLE
GIGGLESWICK
2
Settle Junction

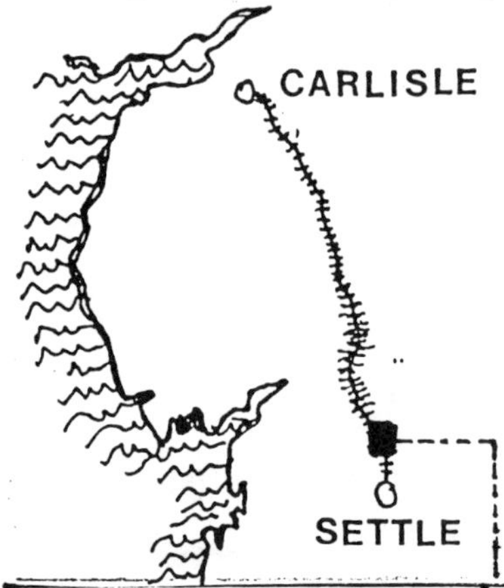
CARLISLE
SETTLE

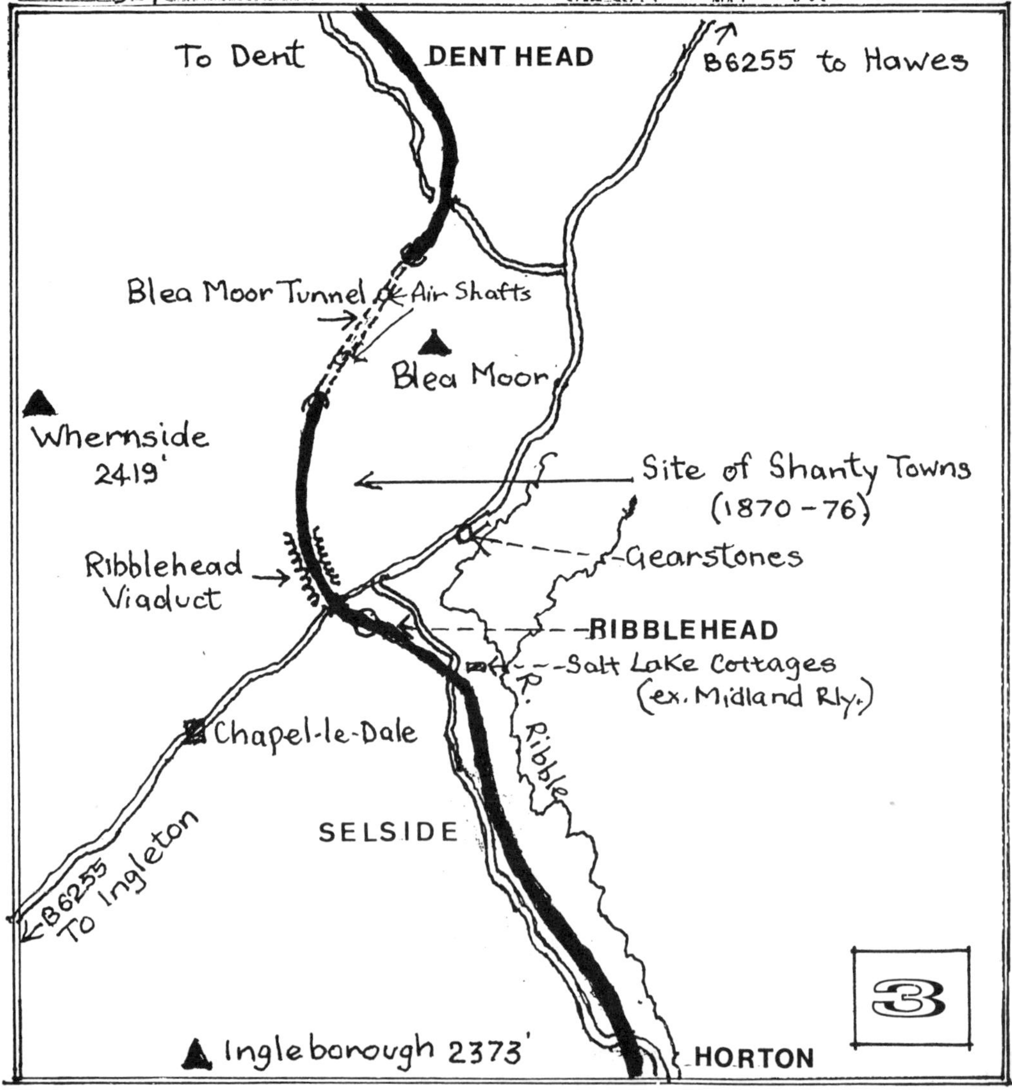
To Dent
DENT HEAD
B6255 to Hawes
Blea Moor Tunnel
Air Shafts
Blea Moor
Whernside
2419'
Site of Shanty Towns
(1870 - 76)
Gearstones
Ribblehead
Viaduct
RIBBLEHEAD
Salt Lake Cottages
(ex. Midland Rly.)
R. Ribble
Chapel-le-Dale
SELSIDE
B6255
To Ingleton
3
Ingleborough 2373'
HORTON

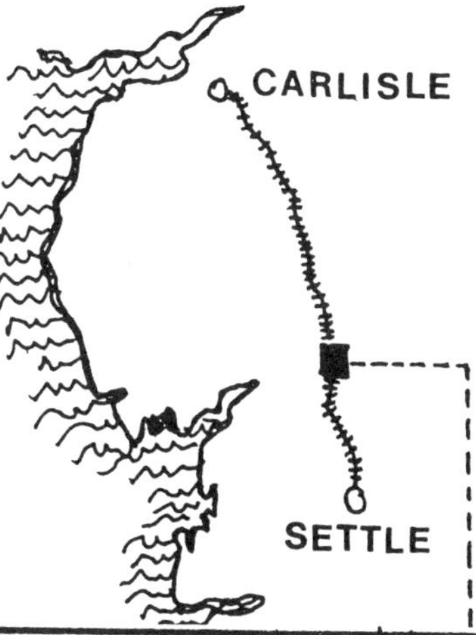
CARLISLE
SETTLE

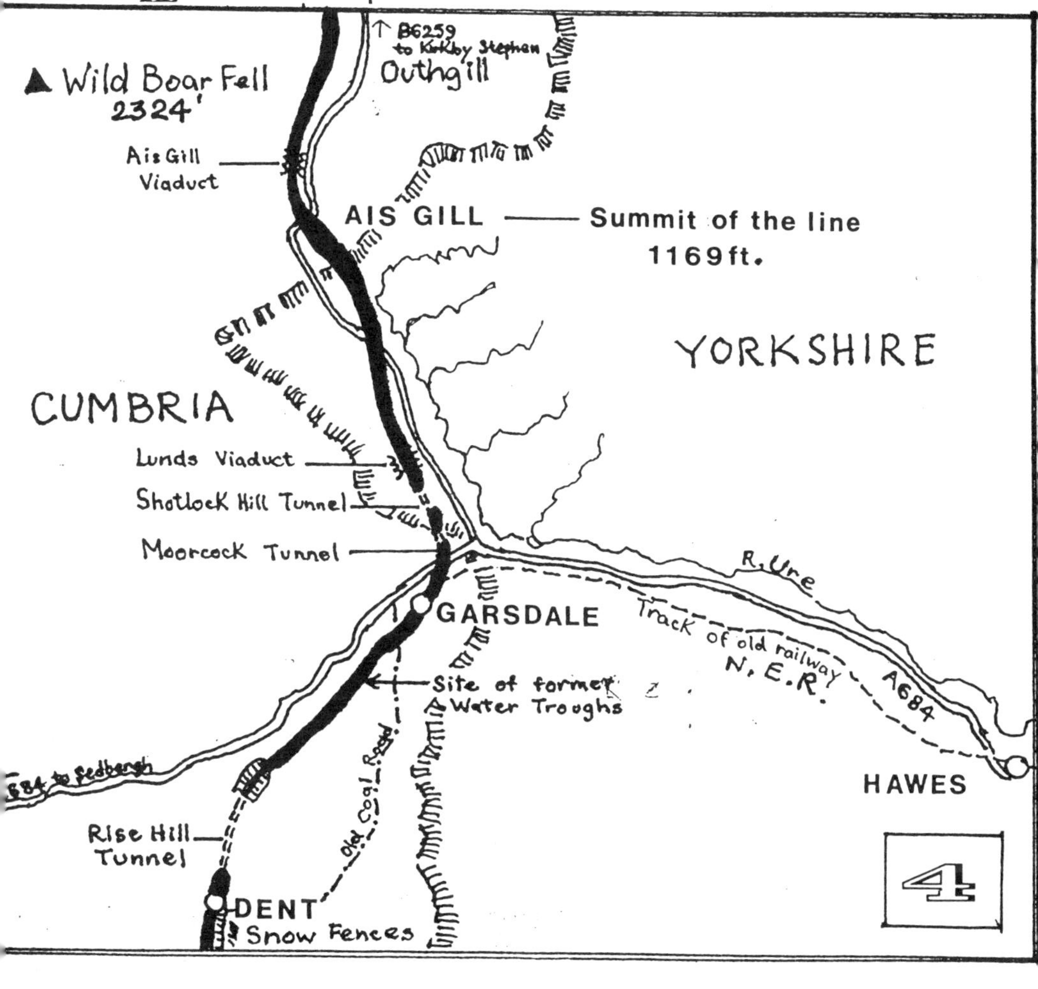
B6259
to Kirkby Stephen
Outhgill
Wild Boar Fell
2324'
Ais Gill
Viaduct
AIS GILL
Summit of the line
1169ft.
YORKSHIRE
CUMBRIA
Lunds Viaduct
Shotlock Hill Tunnel
Moorcock Tunnel
R. Ure
GARSDALE
Track of old railway
N.E.R.
A684
Site of former
Water Troughs
Old Coal Road
684 to Sedbergh
HAWES
Rise Hill
Tunnel
DENT
Snow Fences
4

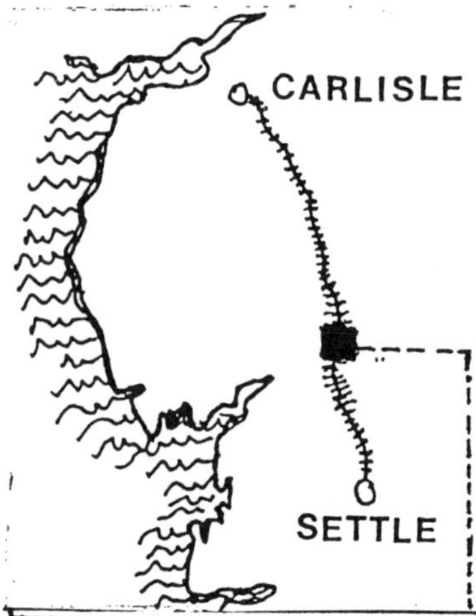
CARLISLE
SETTLE

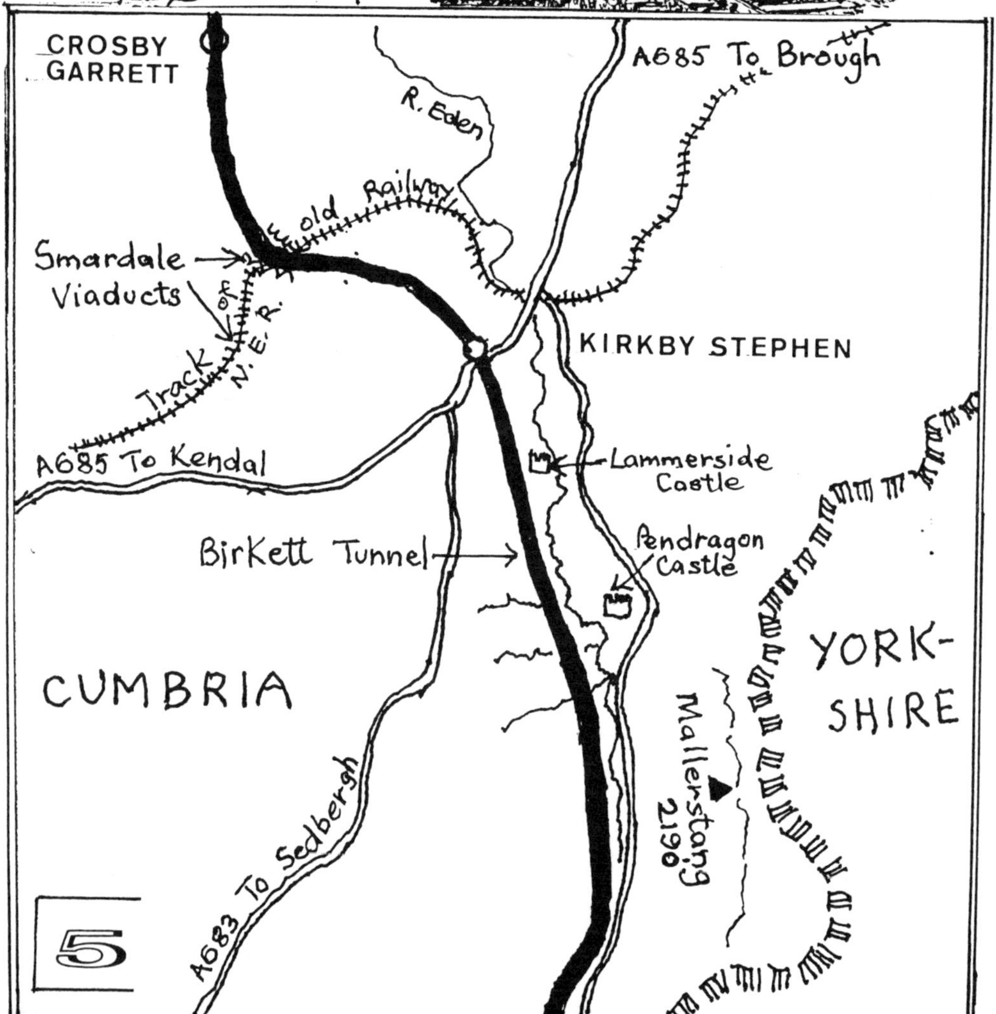
CROSBY GARRETT
A685 To Brough
R. Eden
old Railway
Smardale Viaducts
Track of N.E.R.
KIRKBY STEPHEN
A685 To Kendal
Lammerside Castle
Birkett Tunnel
Pendragon Castle
YORK-SHIRE
CUMBRIA
Mallerstang 2190
A683 To Sedbergh
5

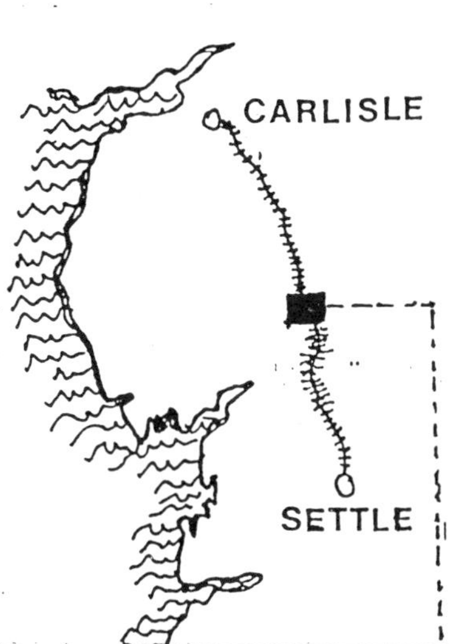
CARLISLE
SETTLE

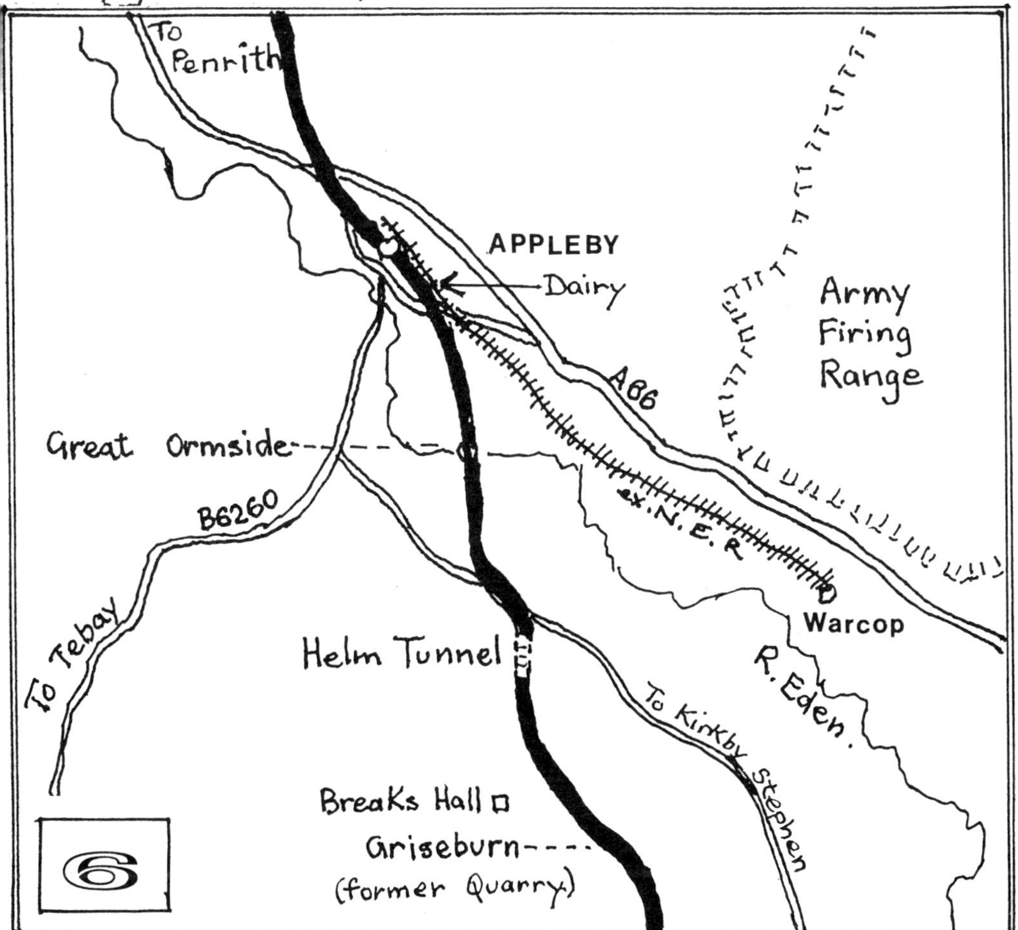
To Penrith
APPLEBY
Dairy
Army Firing Range
A66
Great Ormside
B6260
ex. N. E. R
Warcop
To Tebay
Helm Tunnel
R. Eden.
To Kirkby Stephen
Breaks Hall
Griseburn
(former Quarry)
6

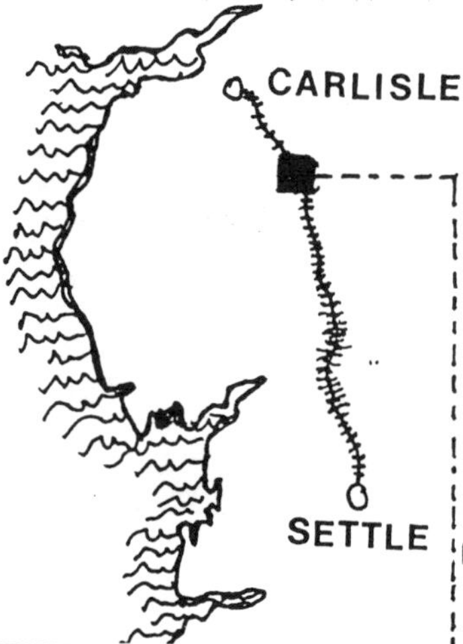
CARLISLE
SETTLE

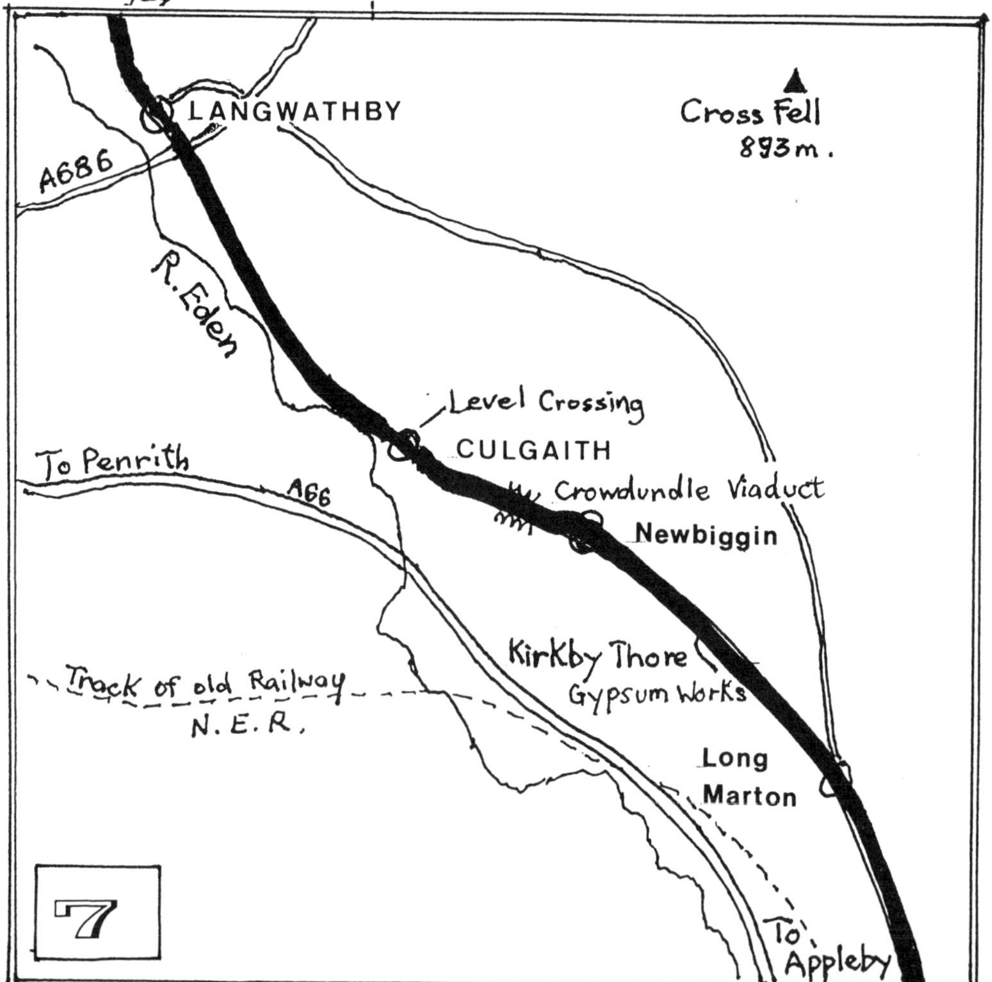
LANGWATHBY
Cross Fell
893m.
A686
R. Eden
Level Crossing
CULGAITH
To Penrith
A66
Crowdundle Viaduct
Newbiggin
Kirkby Thore
Gypsum Works
Track of old Railway
N.E.R.
Long
Marton
To
Appleby
7

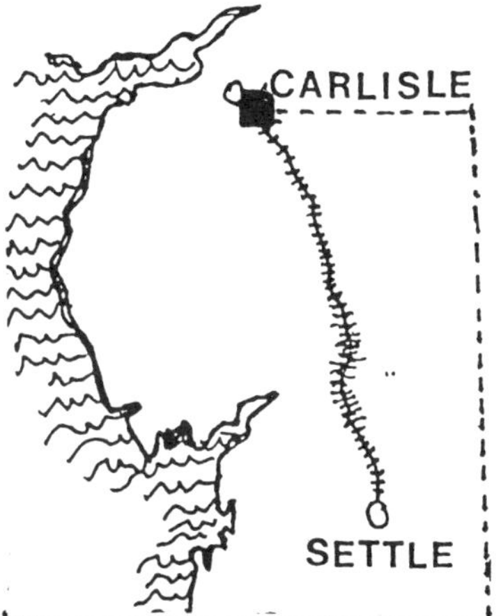
CARLISLE
SETTLE

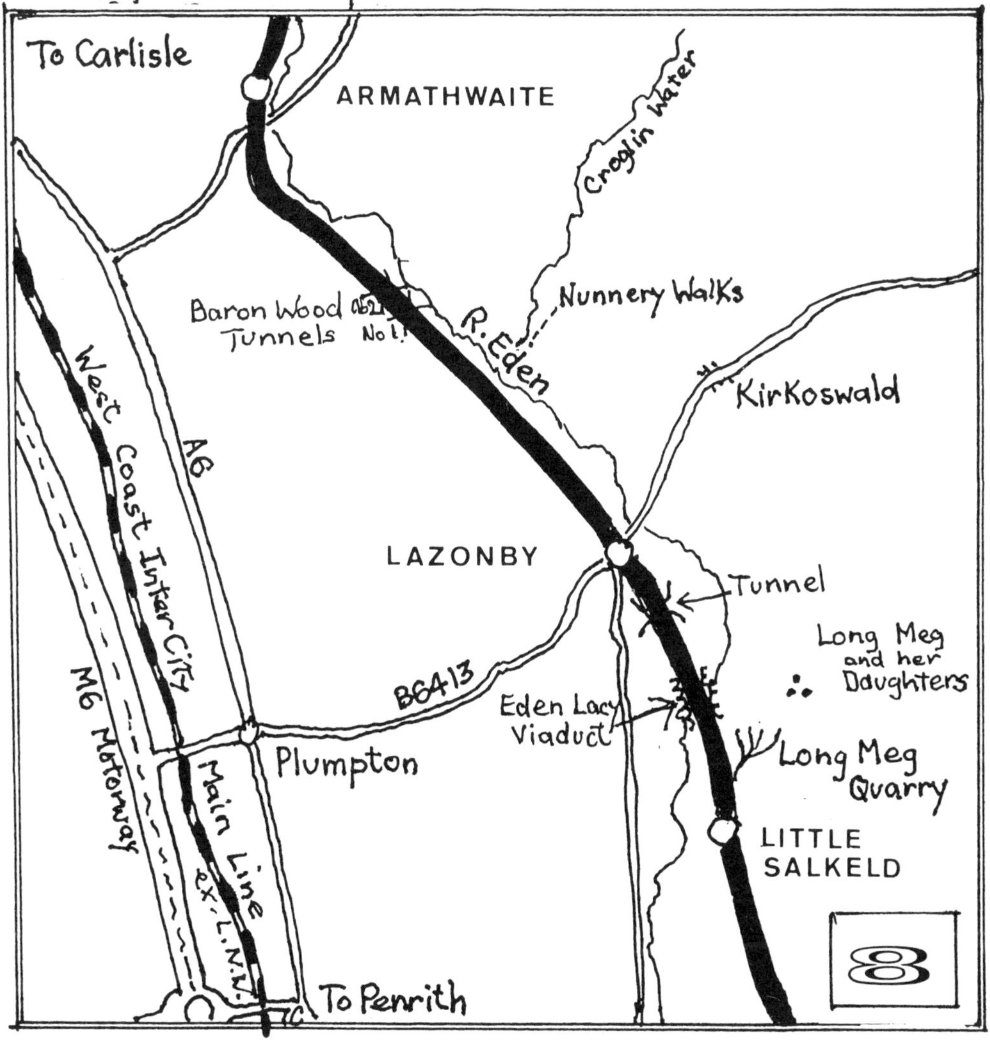
To Carlisle
ARMATHWAITE
Croglin Water
Nunnery Walks
Baron Wood
Tunnels
R. Eden
Kirkoswald
West Coast Inter City
A6
LAZONBY
Tunnel
Long Meg and her Daughters
B6413
Eden Lacy Viaduct
Long Meg Quarry
Plumpton
M6 Motorway
Main Line ex. L.N.W.
LITTLE SALKELD
To Penrith
8

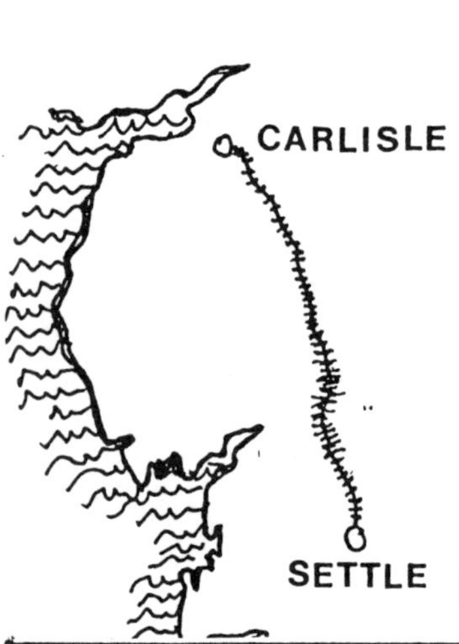
CARLISLE
SETTLE

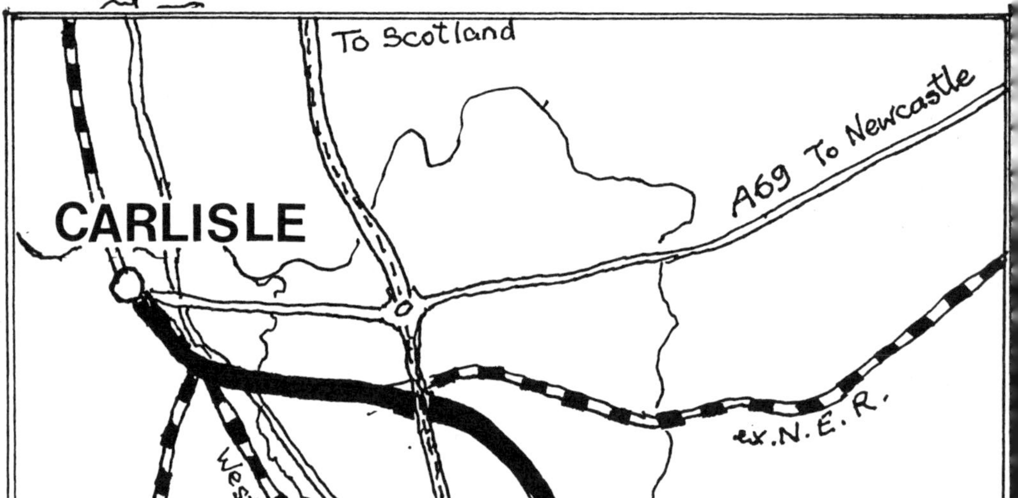
To Scotland
A69 To Newcastle
CARLISLE
ex.N.E.R.
Cumwhinton
West Coast Main Line to London
To Maryport
R. Eden
A6
Cotehill
M6
R. Petteril
To Penrith
Low House L.C.
9
South

A Settle-Carlisle Check List

During a rail journey, there will be little time for reading notes. Keep a check on your travels with reference to this list for the principal attractions between Settle and Carlisle. Use the list in conjunction with the maps. A map number is given against each item, followed by the distance from Carlisle in miles. Travellers from Carlisle to Settle use the simplified list printed in reverse order.

HELLIFIELD (Map 1. 76 3/4). Notice the somewhat narrow signal box at the southern island platform against which the train stops. The line from Lancashire joins from the left. In clear-weather, there will be a glimpse of Pendle Hill, to the west. The famous 'hill of the witches' resembles an upturned boat.

SETTLE JUNCTION (Map 1. 73 1/2). During the short journey from Hellifield, you will have time to look at the broad, shallow Ribble Valley, the river progressing in a series of ox-bows. Large white birds on floodwater could be wintering swans—whooper swans from Iceland. Canada geese may also be seen. The limestone scars (ahead left) are named after Giggleswick. Notice a domed building on a knoll. This is the chapel of Giggleswick School. The Junction signal box has its name proclaimed on the front in old-style lettering. Hereabouts, the Settle-Carlisle begins a 700 ft climb to Blea Moor, with little respite. The ruling gradient is 1 in 100.

SETTLE STATION (Map 2. 71 1/2). The extended platforms are connected by an iron footbridge brought here from Drem, in the North East. The footbridge is a glorious viewpoint, taking in Penyghent and Giggleswick Scars. The unused signal box is to be moved nearer to the station by the Friends of the Settle-Carlisle. In the station yard (right) is a water tank building. The Stationmaster's room has been converted into a shop by the Friends of the Settle-Carlisle line. Two viaducts in Settle itself are Marshfield (6 arches) and Kirkgate (4 arches).

HOFFMAN KILN (Map 2). Where the train emerges from Langcliffe Cutting, look out (right) for the Craven Quarry, now disused, which had a special kiln, named after its German inventor, which enabled the Craven Lime Company to produce limestone continuously, two fires chasing each other round a huge oval structure divided into compartments. The fires were fed by coal from above and drawn round by a draught-control arrangement. Stainforth Tunnel, which passes under the grounds of nearby Taitlands, has a length of 120 yards.

HELWITH BRIDGE (Map 2) is named after five arches, one of which spans the Settle-Carlisle and three crossing the Ribble. The settlement consists of a few dwellings, mostly made of dark flagstone but some of them modern and red-tiled. Quarrying took place for flagstone for domestic and brewing purposes, but is now concerned with roadstone, the big hill on the left (Moughton) bearing quarry scars.

HORTON-IN-RIBBLESDALE (Map 2. 65 1/2). The Stationmaster had supervision of some busy quarry sidings. Horton station was closed in 1970 and re-opened in 1986. The Friends and others have ensured it is kept neat and tidy. Horton station is a great viewpoint for Penyghent (2,272 ft).

RIBBLEHEAD (Map 3. 60 3/4). This station has an isolated, exposed position with an elevation of 1,030 ft. The low, smooth mounds at the head of Ribblesdale are drumlins, a legacy of the final stage of the Ice Age. The station was closed in 1970 and reopened (southbound) in 1986. A northbound platform has now been provided. As the train leaves for Ribblehead Viaduct, look left for a glimpse of flat-topped Ingleborough (2,373 ft), with Whernside (2,419 ft) blocking out half the sky to the north.

BLEA MOOR SIGNAL BOX (Map 3. 59 1/2). This remote box stands at an elevation of 1,100 ft. at the approaches to the south portal of Blea Moor Tunnel, which has a length of 2,629 yards. When the train emerges from Blea Moor, it shortly crosses Dent Head viaduct, of 10 arches, followed soon afterwards by Arten Gill (11 arches) near where is a conspicuous 'green road', heading for Hawes.

DENT STATION (Map 4. 54 3/4). At 1,150 ft, the highest station on the Settle-Carlisle. The station was closed in 1970 and reopened sixteen years later. Notice the up-jutting railway sleepers, forming 'snow fences' and the Stationmaster's House on its knoll. The line runs in a cutting, then on an embankment and, with a Backwoods atmosphere of upstanding conifers, eventually enters Rise Hill Tunnel (1,213 yards).

GARSDALE STATION (Map 4. 51 1/2). A bleak spot, overlooking the head of Garsdale. Much has been ripped out, a notable feature being the turntable (now restored and at the Keighley and Worth Valley line). Notice the large signal box on the 'down' platform. Dandry Mire viaduct, of 12 arches, was the product of second-thought. The original concept was to create an embankment. Look out for solitary Moorcock Inn and a row of railway servants' cottages.

AISGILL (Map 4. 48 1/4). From Dandy Mire viaduct the line crosses viaducts and tunnels, the last-named of modest length. Ahead is the ponderous bulk of Wild Boar Fell (2,324 ft) and, across Mallerstang, Hugh Seat (2,328 ft) named after Hugh de Morville, one of the knights implicated in the murder of Thomas à Becket in Canterbury Cathedral. Aisgill signal box is preserved by the Midland Railway Trust at Butterley in Derbyshire.

MALLERSTANG (Map 5). The railway is on a high ledge, with a view downwards into Mallerstang and across to Mallerstang Edge. Outhgill is the only settlement in the dale, and in the church are embroidered kneelers, each relating to an aspect of local life, including (of course) the railway. A road from near Pendragon Castle passes near the southern portal of Birkett Tunnel (424 yards). Mallerstang terminates with a tract of commonland popular with visitors, including (at Appleby Fair time in June) some of the travelling folk with their horses and hooped caravans.

KIRKBY STEPHEN (Map 5. 41 1/2). The Midland station, perched at an elevation of 890 ft, and a mile and a-half from town, was closed in 1970 and re-opened in 1986. From Kirkby Stephen the line enters glorious limestone country. Smardale is crossed by a 12-arch viaduct which is also the tallest on the line. At Crosby Garrett, little beyond basic railway structures remain of a busy station. To the north is the halfway point between Settle Junction and Petteril Bridge Junction, at Carlisle. Helm Beck is crossed by the seven-arch Griseburn viaduct and Helm Tunnel keeps the railway out of the eye of the sun for 571 yards.

ORMSIDE (Map 6. 33 1/4) is not far from Warcop, a redstone village where the Army is Lord of Manor, having acquired this with property they converted into a vast firing range. Ormside station has been closed since 1952. Ormside viaduct, to the north, crosses the River Eden with 10 majestic arches.

APPLEBY (Map 6. 30 3/4) is one of the major stations on the Settle-Carlisle line with long platforms, a metal footbridge and a water crane installed in recent times to service 'steam specials'. Bishop Treacy, of Wakefield, who had a passion for railway photography, died at Appleby in 1978.

LONG MARTON (Map 7. 28). The station closed in 1970. Nearby are busy commercial sidings, serving the gypsum works at Kirkby Thore. In vew now is Cross Fell, the highest of the Pennne hills. Nearby are the sidings of Kirkby Thore gypsum works. To the west is Lakeland. To the east, the long Pennine ridge, including Cross Fell (2,930 ft) and Great Dun Fell (with the radomes).

NEW BIGGIN (Map 7. 24 3/4). The station closed in 1970. Some of the old station buildings have been adapted as dwellings. Nearby Crowdundle viaduct is, like other structures in these parts, built of new red sandstone. The four arches of the viaduct carry it acoss a beck flowing down from the Pennines.

CULGAITH (Map 7. 23 1/2). A level crossing is controlled by a signalbox. Nearby is a garden centre, with a cafe adorned with railway material and photographs. The station closed in 1970 but the buildings remain,. Up the track can be seen the south portal of Culgaith tunnel (661 yards) with, a little further, Waste Bank tunnel (164 yards). The train emerges from this tunnel in an area where the view opens up to take in the fertile flatlands where the Eamont (from Ullswater, a distance of nine miles) blends its water with the Eden.

LANGWATHBY (Map 7. 19 3/4). The station closed in 1970 and reopened in 1986. In the main building is a cafe with the name *Brief Encounter*.

LITTLE SALKELD (Map 8. 18 1/2). The station closed in 1970. A little to the north is Long Meg signal box, which was associated with the Long Meg mines (anhydrite). On high ground to the east of the village is a famous stone circle, Long Meg and her Daughters. Eden Lacy viaduct crosses the Eden with 7 arches.

LAZONBY AND KIRKOSWALD (Map 8. 15 1/2). Closed in 1970, the station reopened in 1986 and much of it is now owned and used by a firm of bakers. The adjacent inn is the Midland, after the railway company. Lazonby mart, which is famous for the quality of hillgoing sheep offered here in autumn, is near at hand.

ARMATHWAITE (Map 8. 10). The line runs on a ledge to the west of the Eden Gorge, a well-wooded area which has affinities—pines, heather and deer—with Scotland. Before Armathwaite is reached, the line goes through two tunnels named Baron Wood, through Armathwaite tunnel (325 yards) and across a viaduct of nine arches. Armathwaite station was closed but reopened in 1986. To the north is seven-arch Dry Beck viaduct and Low House, one of two road level crossings on the Settle-Carlisle. (The other is at Culgaith).

CUMWHINTON (Map 9. 4). The station is closed; so is that at Scotby, one and a-quarter miles to the north. The Settle-Carlisle joins the west coast main line at Petteril Bridge Junction.

CARLISLE (Map 9. 0). Known as Carlisle Citadel, the station was opened in 1847 and later extended. Seven railway companies, among them the Midland, operated from it.

A List of Some Features to be looked for between Carlisle and Settle

LOW HOUSE CROSSING

BARON WOOD TUNNELS

LAZONBY AND KIRKOSWALD

EDEN LACY VIADUCT

LONG MEG SIGNAL BOX

LITTLE SALKELD

LANGWATHBY

CULGAITH TUNNEL

CULGAITH SIGNAL BOX

CROWDUNDLE VIADUCT

NEW BIGGIN

LONG MARTON

APPLEBY STATION

ORMSIDE VIADUCT

ORMSIDE STATION

GRISEBURN VIADUCT

CROSBY GARRETT

SMARDALE VIADUCT

KIRKBY STEPHEN

BIRKETT TUNNEL

AISGILL

GRISEDALE CROSSING

LUNDS VIADUCT

MOORCOCK TUNNEL

DANDRY MIRE VIADUCT

GARSDALE

RISE HILL TUNNEL

DENT STATION

ARTENGILL VIADUCT

DENT HEAD VIADUCT

BLEA MOOR TUNNEL

BLEA MOOR SIGNAL BOX

RIBBLEHEAD VIADUCT

RIBBLEHEAD STATION

HORTON-IN-RIBBLESDALE

STAINFORTH TUNNEL

SETTLE STATION

SETTLE JUNCTION

LONG PRESTON STATION

HELLIFIELD

Features On The Way

Hellifield Station

Though strictly not a Settle-Carlisle station, Hellifield is a key junction, linked with Lancashire via Clitheroe and Blackburn. Efforts have been made over several years to bring back some kind of regular passenger service from Clitheroe to Hellifield.

A rail traveller immediately notices an ornate station canopy, gloriously restored, with the Midland Railway monograph and its emblem, the wyvern, which is usually mistaken for a dragon. A visitor to Hellifield station approaches the island platforms via a miserable tiled subway.

The joint station was opened in 1880. Hellifield, with an engine shed housing 28 locomotives, plus two snow ploughs; with carriage sheds, cattle docks and sidings, was at its peak of usage from about 1900 to 1914, and at its busiest handled almost 200,000 goods wagons a year. Harry Speight, the late Victorian topographer, wrote that "the rather elevated and windy position of the station on the edge of Hellifield Moor is not calculated to 'jubilate' the traveller on a raw night. There is, however, ample waiting-room accommodation, a book stall and a refreshment room." Hellifield lost its passenger service in 1962 and its freight services in 1964. Both were to be revived and the island station itself, with its splendid wrought-iron canopy, restored. Hellifield now has the promise of a bright future, with a new approach road, revived facilities and plans for a new engine shed.

When Hellifield had three signal boxes (with a total of 112 levers), man might at one time or another experience working them all. The north box controlled traffic for the loops and also the carriage sidings, as well as the Dump (engineer's sidings). The south box had oversight of the junction, plus shunting on the high sidings and the points going into the shed.

The old Lancashire and Yorkshire box, which stood on the embankment near the road bridge, was related to low level sidings, where the cattle dock was situated. Being an old 'Lanky' box, it had a frame which was level with the ground. Its position on an embankment ensured it was draughty and a signalman would spend part of his time lagging it with oddments of carpet to keep out the wind.

Hellifield had back-up facilities for the Settle-Carlisle. A 30 ton crane was available for lifting heavy loads, such as girders from a wagon with hot axle-bearings or for dealing with a derailment. The crane was not kept in steam. Those who manned it were often stoking it up as they travelled to an incident. Hellifield cattle market, which came into being in the 1880s, made good use of the cattle dock, which by the turn of the century was handling over 1,000 wagons a year. Seven years later, the figure was 1,512 wagons.

There was the usual station smell compounded of fish and soot. Fish consigned by rail from Scotland in boxes containing ice arrived at Hellifield with the ice melted. The guard had usually sprinkled the smelly water with sawdust from a box kept under his seat in the brake van.

Early this century, the refreshment room was run by a manageress with the help of three waitresses, a cook and cellarman. A lad was employed to take a tray holding fruit and chocolates to people on the train. Luncheon baskets were also available. The same lad spent hours washing up, collecting the dirty trays and pots via a four-wheeled barrow. Washing-up took place in a large bath which stood in the cellar. The refreshment room staff maintained a good fire. It was not unknown for a driver or fireman to "bring a bit o' good coal in" when he called for a snack. The catering staff had accommodation above the refreshment room. Cooking facilities were also at the higher floor, the hot meals and baked items being delivered by hoist to the waitresses below.

Settle Junction

At the approach to the Junction, a passenger's eyes stray to the broad shallow valley of the Ribble which in winter is frequently flooded and clouded with waterfowl and wading birds. On the map, the ox-bows of the river look like doodles. Earthen banks restrain the river but springs on either side of the valley soon cause fields to be inundated.

Settle Junction signal box heralds the start of the Settle-Carlisle with the tracks swinging away from the old Morecambe line. Settle Junction passenger station (1876-1877) was short-lived. So, too, was a roadside barrier of wooden sleepers intended to avoid horses on the main road being startled by the passage of steam trains.

The present signal box was erected in 1913 and is therefore a genuine Midland structure, though the frame was replaced in 1959. Electricity is installed and Calor gas available for cooking. Water for drinking and washing is brought from Skipton in two gallon cans.

In its heyday, Settle Junction box kept the signalman "on his toes". Even in the early 1950s, there might be from fifteen to twenty trains bound for Morecambe alone. The duty man reckoned that if he had not cleaned up the box by 9am he would not be able to do it until after dinner.

Settle

Three sizes of station were used and the largest size was selected for Settle, Kirkby Stephen and Appleby. The style has been called 'Derby Gothic'. Notice at Settle that the basic design is of twin pavilions separated by a glazed front porch through which passengers enter the building. All stations were fitted with ornamental bargeboards at their gable ends and with a trefoil device on the upper walls.

In the case of Settle, these recesses provide snug quarters for mice—Mickey and Minnie, plastic models of Disney creations. The former, found nailed to a telegraph pole at Dent station, over 1,000 feet above sea level, was brought down to sub-tropical Settle and given snug quarters. In due course he was joined by Minnie. At Christmas-time, a decorated tree stands in the entrance hall and sherry and mice pies are served in the waiting room by Friends as three French horn players, members of the orchestra of Opera North, provide a music accompaniment to eating and convivial chattering.

At Settle, the lines are spanned by a rainbow arch—a brightly painted cast iron bridge, brought here from Drem, on the East Coast main line. Settle Station, complete with goods yard and shed, was built in 'gothic' style of Bradford stone. The site was levelled by the tipping of a vast quantity of material. Settle is the proverbial shadow of its former self. Much of the old goods area, which had a shed and coal sidings, is now occupied by small industrial units under the generic term The Sidings.

Originally, the water supply for the station came from Stainforth, flowing in a lineside channel, to be stored in a large iron tank until needed for the station, the toilets and the water column at the platform end. The farmer at Stainforth submitted a water bill at regular intervals. If the Midland was slow to settle the account, he simply diverted the water away from the railway. Paraffin (delivered weekly from Skipton) was needed for the station buildings and for the signal lamps. Each week a lamp unit, container and burner, was replaced by one which was full and had a neatly trimmed wick.

Porters of the 1930s had a hectic round. The first train, the 'workman's', was well patronised to Horton-in-Ribblesdale, departing from Settle at 6.20am with a goodly number of quarrymen. The first train on Saturday was the 7.20 to Leeds. There was someone on duty at Settle until 10.30, when the last train departed for Leeds. On Saturday, the last train was the 11.45 to Hellifield, a stopping place for express trains. This train was known as the Ghost Train at Settle because when it arrived there was no one on it!.

In the autumn, local farmers travelled to Hawes or Kirkby Stephen for their tups, returning on the train with them. If anyone entered the guard's van on the express, he or she might come under the withering gaze of a fretful tup. A farmer with stock to transport rang the station in advance and booked a cattle wagon—large, medium or small. Thrifty men usually wanted a small van, into which the cows would have to be squeezed.

Virtually everything used in the Settle district arrived by rail. For example, Mr Lord the greengrocer, having been to Bradford to buy in the wholesale market, had the produce conveyed to Forster Square station for despatch by train to Settle. The produce was transported to Lord's shop on a four-wheeled platform barrow. On Tuesday, market day, the incoming passengers included farmers' wives with baskets containing home produce—butter, cheese, eggs—which they sold to local grocers or bartered for necessities, which were then taken back by rail.

Also at Settle, a cattle dock of twelve pens was well used. Irish cattle were collected by a drover—perhaps Old Mick, nicknamed the 'bull-walloper'—and taken to the rear of a local hotel where they were put up for sale. The station staff occasionally pursued a cow bolting for freedom. Railway employees also knew the frustration of collecting pigs from local rearers. They had been bought by a Halifax man who now wished them to be transported to his premises by train.

The 'coal road' had been installed for the benefit of five coal merchants who dealt with both domestic coal and coke. Most of the coal was delivered from South Yorkshire collieries to Hector Christie, a local mill owner, and to the Settle Gas Company. The many private coal wagons had the owners' names displayed, among the names being John Delaney, a quarry tycoon, Charles John Lord and Jim Capstick.

Settle Station's 'feel good' factor has been intensified by winning best-kept station awards and by the opening of a shop manned by the Friends. This has brought into full use the Stationmaster's Office, with its fireplace of Dent Marble. The Friends of the Settle-Carlisle reached agreement with *Railtrack* to move the redundant signalbox at Settle station nearer to the platforms for restoration and eventual opening to the public.

Stainforth Siding

The embankment north of Settle provides a good vantage point for the district. Behind Settle, the limestone cliff of Castleberg is fringed with trees. A fault line (displacement of the earth, now separating on the surface millstone grit from limestone) passes through the town. The limestone to the north is part of the largest outcrop of this pearl-white rock in Britain. A domed building on a gritstone knoll just beyond Giggleswick is not an observatory but the chapel of Giggleswick School.

After the constriction of Langcliffe cutting, the viewpoint widens to take in a limestone cliff, the well-weathered face of a redundant quarry once run by the Craven Lime Company. It was the first quarry to be developed to take advantage of the Settle-Carlisle and lime was being transported from it, southwards to the Bradford district in 1873, before the railway in its entirety had been opened for freight traffic in 1876.

A Hoffman kiln, devised for continuous burning of limestone, was installed, the numbers 1876 being set in white against the red brickwork of a lofty chimney. The Hoffman became disused in the 1930s. The kiln itself survives and is to be preserved as the centrepiece of a visitor centre.

The standard Midland box of 1898, with its 16 lever tumbler frame, was replaced in 1950 by a wooden box based on LMS design—a box which was badly damaged by derailed wagons in 1961 and 1963. On the second occasion, Mr Wilson the signalman was not amused when it was suggested that an ejector seat should be fitted. The box was removed not long after the second accident.

Stainforth Tunnel

A modest 120 yards, it passes under Taitlands, a mini-mansion, the owners of which were given an expenses-paid leave of absence by the Midland men during the explosive period of tunnel-making. Taitlands is now a youth hostel.

Sheriff Brow Viaduct

A viaduct not appreciated by those who travel over it because of the grand surroundings and little-known to visitors because there is no right of way beside it. The graceful skew stone-built structure is in a gorge of the Ribble where the river had its course re-shaped to accommodate the line in its 1 in 100 gradient.

Helwith Bridge

The Settle-Carlisle, having crossed Sheriff Brow viaduct, passes through the Ribble gorge and comes in sight of Five Arches bridge, a structure from which a small quarrying settlement took its name. The half-mile of track between Five Arches and Crag Hill Farm is untypically level.

A signal box which stood to the east of the Ribble controlled quarry traffic. Five little quarries used to supply flagstone for use domestically, as floor covering, shelves in dairies and sections of water-cisterns, collecting rainwater from the roof. Eventually, quarrying was switched from flags to roadstone. Notice a dramatic change in the appearance of Moughton Hill. One quarry, on being closed, filled with water and is now a fishery.

High on Moughton is an Unconformity, where the upjutting flagstone supports the horizontal layers of limestone, which was quarried at the felltop, the rock being transported by incline railway on an endless band, the laden wagons going down drawing up the empties. The Foredale Quarry was known as Nibble.

The half-mile of track between Five Arches and Crag Hill farm is the only level stretch of track on the 22 miles of the Long Drag.

Horton-in-Ribblesdale

The station, one of the 'small' variety, has been renovated by the Friends of the Settle-Carlisle. The Midland signal box remained inactive, unconnected for a few years until it burnt down in mysterious circumstances.

Horton station served the local people, including farmers who took advantage of the presence of three cattle pens. These were inadequate in autumn, when a special train hired by Craven flockmasters ran from Bell Busk to the Eden Valley, where sheep were wintered in the rootfields. One of the collection points was Horton, sheep converging on the station from as far away as Old Ing, at the dalehead. The stocks had to be kept separate; hence the sight of shepherds and their dogs keeping them more or less contained while the railway porters loaded.

At Horton, the Settle-Carlisle was linked by sidings to the big Beecroft Quarry, which in the 1950s dealt with a quarter of a million tons of incoming coal and outgoing lime each year. Lime was transported mainly for use as a flux in the Scottish steel industry and for surfacing roads. Banking between forty and fifty empty wagons at Horton could be spectacular. The train was drawn out of the station, beyond the starting signal, and then the signalman turned the points. There were two roads up—a front and a back road—and the empties used the former so it was vital that the points were set correctly.

The driver took the train well up the line. The shunter, after ensuring all was well, tipped off the Stationmaster, who alerted the locomotive driver. He opened the regulater fully and—*WHAM: clank, clank, clank, clank, clank! zzzzz!* The deed was done or, if it failed, it was attempted again. If there were derailments, the Hellifield steam crane was summoned.

The guard on Old Limey had to be especially alert during the main line journey. With a train consisting of seventy wagons of lime, it was vital to keep the couplings tight on the gradients and to brake when Aisgill was reached and the train was on the long descent to Appleby, where the now thirsty locomotive was watered.

Station pride had a late flowering when J M Taylor was Stationmaster. He and his staff created a prize-winning station garden. They simply hacked up part of the platform, without going through the 'usual channels' for permission. They won the station garden competition for 17 years. Exhibitions were organised in the waiting room. Horton was closed to goods traffic in 1965, then re-opened in 1986. To mark this tenth anniversary, the Friends recreated the display and nameboards on the southbound platform. The northbound waiting shelter was refurbished and the gardens brought back to something of the condition which existed in Jim Taylor's day.

Selside

The signal box is now at Steamtown, Carnforth. At Selside, it had been brought into use in 1907, to break up the 'block system', having only two levers one way and two levers the other. As a link, Selside saved delays, especially in bad weather. The box was closed in 1975. During the 1939-45 war, Selside was the only mainline signalbox manned round the clock by women. A amusing incident concerns the driver of a locomotive who, held up by the signal, entered the box. His mission was misconstrued when he said to the signalwoman: "Get 'em off." He was referring to the signals, of course.

Salt Lake Cottages

A terrace of six cottages, built for 'railway servants' but privatised, has the curious name of Salt Lake because, some say, a shanty stood here during construction days. No historical evidence of a shanty has so far been found. The name probably became familiar during missionary work by Mormons from Salt Lake City, Utah. They were known to be seeking converts in the Dales in the 1860s.

The row of dwellings is typical of those erected by the Midland to house railway servants, as they were then known. Three double-sided projecting porches give them a touch of distinction. A former resident recalls the cottages as being exposed to wind and rain. Thunderstorms were protracted, as though they were circling the hills. In 1947. when The Big Snow was experienced, the children of Salt Lake were unable to attend school at Chapel-le-Dale or Ingleton for eight weeks. A train service of sorts was operated as far as Ribblehead. At Salt Lake, a 'snow platform' was built. The local people walked over the snow directly into the train. The driver of one train asked a Salt Laker if she wanted some 'black snow'. If so, she should fetch a sack. He filled it with coal.

Lily Towler, who went to No.3 Salt Lake on her marriage in 1932, recalls that the rent of 5s a week was deducted from the wage of her husband, Jack, and that left an income of £1.30s a week. Coal arrived at Ribblehead station and was distributed by Jack Preston of Ingleton. Provisions were obtained from visiting tradespeople, including t'Co-op from Settle. Free passes on the railway ensured cheap trips to Settle for shopping once a week, on a Tuesday, when it was market day. A trip to Settle on Saturday was by 'privilege ticket', which meant paying quarter fare.

It was six mile round trip from Salt Lake to St. Leonard's Church, Chapel-le-Dale. The Salt Lakers thus attended periodic services in the waiting room at Ribblehead station, which was attended by the Vicar of Ingleton. He used a back-rest at the ticket office as a lectern. The idea of holding a service here came from Joe Shepherd, stationmaster.

Mrs Towler's recollections of Salt Lake would apply in general to the many other rows of cottages to be found alongside the Settle-Carlisle. Three bedrooms, a living room, kitchen and pantry were the principal accommodation, the kitchen holding an average family at mealtimes. On one wall was the fireplace, flanked by oven and side boiler in the traditional way, the whole given a shine if not a sparkle by a weekly application of black lead. The oven was used for baking—bread, teacakes or scones, nowt fancy or expensive. In the case of Salt Lake, water was carried from a spring beyond the bridge spanning the railway. In the yard of each house was a range of outhouses, one with a set-pot for washing purposes. On wash-day, a set-boiler was filled with water and a fire made of bits of old sleepers and coal. Washing was aided by rubbing board, posser and a mangle with wooden rollers. Clothes which had been dried and ironed were 'aired' on a wooden rack suspended from the kitchen ceiling.

Lily Towler recalls when a cow entered her house. "It was Monday. Nine o' clock. Just after the kiddies had gone to school. I was getting the clothes ready in the wash-house.

And, of course, I'd left the back gate open. A farm man was driving the cows up the back lane into the field. Then I noticed that one cow was walking into my house by the back door. I screamed. The farm man came, but not before the cow had entered my sitting room and had come out again. The man said it was a wonder it had not tried to leave by jumping through the window. I said it was a wonder if had not done anything on the floor. If it had, he would have had to clean up!''

When the cottages were sold in the 1950s, each was valued at £100. The sitting tenants had 'first refusal', but none responded. All the cottages are now privately owned.

Ribblehead Station

The smaller type of station was built at Ribblehead, where the Settle-Carlisle leaves Ribblesdale and begins its high fell-wandering. The name first chosen for the station was Batty Green. A modification to the normal Midland style, in a wild, wet situation, was the addition of tiles to the end and projecting gables. (Similar protection was afforded the *Station Inn,* which is situated just across the road from the drive leading to the railway station).

The view eastwards takes in the road, formerly the Lancaster-Richmond turnpike, extending towards a huddle of buildings called Gearstones, an inn in 'railway time', the high ground beyond being Cam End. From the platforms of Ribblehead may be viewed the 'drumlin' field of the upper Ribble, mighty Whernside (the highest fell in the Yorkshire Dales National Park) and Park Fell, leading on to flat-topped Ingleborough.

Several stationmasters (and, latterly, before the station became an unstaffed halt, the wife of one of them) sustained a tradition of sending coded details of the weather, on the hour, to the Air Ministry. Frederick W Houghton, writing in 1948, observed: ''Ribblehead is a particularly windy spot and no one who has stood on that gale-whipped platform needs to ask why this station has been chosen as a meteorological report point.'' The height of the cloud base could usually be assessed in relation to the summits of nearby fells, but when in doubt the Stationmaster would release a hydrogen-filled balloon and note the duration of its climb to cloud base, knowing that the balloon was ascending at 400 feet per minute.

The station was closed to passengers with the withdrawal of local services. There began a steady deterioration in the property. The main waiting room became a billet for railway works, who cat-napped or warmed up pies on a stove. With the return of the local service, the southbound platform only was able to be used, the northbound having been demolished to improve access to the limestone quarry. At the station, slates slithered from the roof, leaving rents through which timbers showed like the ribs of a dead sheep.

In 1986, local services were reinstated. A northbound platform, complete with shelter (and heating facility), was brought into use in 1993. The cost was met not by British Rail but by donations from charities and organisations, including the Friends of the Settle-Carlisle. In 1997, there are plans to restore the building, which will house an interpretive display about both the Settle-Carlisle and the Ribblehead area.

Ribblehead Viaduct

The rail traveller is scarcely aware of Ribblehead viaduct. There is just the sensation of height. Viewed from a distance at ground level and this viaduct, its embankments like gigantic book-ends, come into the American 'gee whiz' category.

Those who use the nearby road regularly comment on the ever-changing appearance, related to the passing of the seasons, the time of day and its effect on the shadow pattern of the immense piers. There are special effects, as in mist, when the high arches are a mysterious dove-grey.

Ribblehead viaduct, the most conspicuous structure on the Settle-Carlisle, is basically the standard Midland viaduct in a special fell-country setting. To the Settle-Carlisle engineers, it is simply Bridge 66. They are familiar with what one of them called 'the Ribblehead factor', which is a Pennine cocktail of driving rain, wind and mist. Among the great viaducts of this railway, Arten Gill is more impressive, but that is tucked away in the upper valley of the Dee. Smardale is big and so tall it seems to be standing on tiptoe but is seen by just few intrepid visitors who follow a network of little roads near Kirkby Stephen. Ribblehead almost shouts to be noticed.

The basic details mean little by themselves—440 yards long, 104 ft maximum height, 24 arches. But stand beside Pier 13, where a memorial was raised to workers old and new, and the scale is cathedral-like. Ribblehead is a composite structure, made of dark limestone, the arches turned in brick. A strip of millstone grit, somewhat yellowish in tone, is also detectable high on the structure.

To the east of the viaduct is a tortured stretch of ground where stood various hutments, lime kiln and brickworks. Notice the 'green track' leading northwards, towards the scars, this being what remains of the tramway which in the construction period connected the various working areas and what have become grandly known as 'shanty towns'.

Local people say the viaduct was 'built on wool'. In fact, it rests in concrete above bedrock. Ribblehead viaduct, which is 120 years old, has been designated an 'ancient monument'. The gods of the Pennine weather give the area turbulance. Gale force winds of over 100 miles an hour are recorded periodically. In November, 1961, the Ribblehead anemometer recorded a wind speed of 92 miles an hour and planks on the scaffolding erected for maintenance work were said to ''go up and down like piano keys''.

Seepage of rainwater, not the notorious wind, led to the viaduct being given an expensive restoration in the 1990s. In a face-lift consisting £3 million, the deck was waterproofed (1990) and the remaining part of the structure restored in the following year. Cores taken by the engineers included one of brickwork under the arches, revealing the nature of those made locally, using clay. An old record that they 'rang like pots' should not be trusted. Ribblehead bricks were porous, speckled with 'foreign bodies'. Within a short time of construction, much of the original brickwork was replaced with a harder engineering brick—either Staffordshire blue or Accrington red.

Blea Moor

Having crossed Ribblehead viaduct, the train heads for Blea Moor, which has a quite ordinary shape, something like an upturned porridge basin. What appear to be large sores on the face of Blea Moor are heaps of debris, from pebbles to huge stones, drawn painstakingly up the shafts from where miners were blasting through the Moor to create a 2,629 yard long tunnel.

The walker from Ribblehead finds him/herself in an area of gritstone and peat, with coarse grasses everywhere and a little heather remaining on the dry ridges. In spring, lapwings tumble in the air and wail like lost spirits. Sheep stare mournfully at passers-by. Years ago, when there were fewer sheep and more heather - also, incidentally, lots of grouse - sparks from a passing steam locomotive would ignite the heather. The fire was usually allowed to burn itself out.

Railwaywise, this is an impoverished area. The water column has gone. In keen weather, travellers saw a cheery patch where a stove was being stoked up to prevent the column from freezing-up. A signal box remains, but the big tank house has gone. So have most of the houses which stood up here. There is a solitary patch of Blea Moor rhubarb (which is sour and pithy) in what used to be a garden.

In 1941, the rail facilities at Blea Moor were extended to create passing loops, which replaced the lie-by sidings. Once some wagons on a monkey-muck (iron ore) train at Blea Moor ran away when a sudden jerk which occurred while one was being manoevred at Blea Moor broke the coupling. Eighteen wagons began the long, free run towards the Ribble Valley and stopped of their own accord near Long Preston. The same thing happened to some covered wagons of an ammunition train.

Blea Moor was the area where railway maintenance men were on bad-weather duty. A store of between 30 and 40 new wagon sheets was kept hereabouts to replace any which the gales whipped from the wagons of goods trains during the crossing of Ribblehead viaduct. A sheet was heavy but with a gale behind it would float across country for up to half a mile, looking for all the world like a wind-blown leaf. All the local farmers had one or two airborne sheets which came to earth on their holdings.

The driver of a goods train who did not want to gamble on being able to replenish the reserves of water at the Garsdale troughs usually went 'inside' at Blea Moor to fill his tank at the water column. When a gale was rampaging across the district, a major task was keeping the leather nozzle in the neck of the tank. Then the fireman would wrap his arms around it, as though he was loving it.

Blea Moor Signal Box

The first signal box, on the 'down' side, was replaced in 1941 by a new brick and timber LMS box of 30 levers. This is the box in current use, standing beside the 'up' line. With a left hand frame, the signalman faces the back wall, not the front windows, when he is working. (The change in the position and type of signal box occurred when the track arrangement was changed from back-in siding on up and down lines into facing loops).

Paraffin, needed for the lamps, was delivered in a large drum which was rolled into the lamp house. A platelayer or porter would bring the lamps to the box and was held responsible for replacing them. Clambering up a signal on a wet day to exchange an almost empty lamp for one which was fully charged was not a pleasant job. An ordinary lamp lasted for about four days, though the lamp at the distant signal was larger and could be replaced at weekly intervals.

A lamp position inside the box gave poor light. It was maintained by the railway bosses that if there was too much light in the box the signalman would not be able to see what was going on outside. Not a great deal was visible at night, even in the days when traffic was incessant. There would perhaps be just the glow from a hot axle-box on a passing train. One signalman who regarded his job with levity and humour referred to Blea Moor tunnel as the 'Toob', even when reporting to Control. He applied for a vacancy at Garsdale but failed on the telegraph instrument, while claiming that if an instrument could be found with a rubber needle (presumably to erase his errors) he would pass.

The shell of a house is all that remains of Blea Moor Cottages, built to accommodate railway workers in an otherwise remote area. Children sometimes walked across the viaduct on their way to school. On a windy day, they forced over the parapets some blue grocery bags they had blown up. They hoped the wind would take a bag under the arch and return it via the other side. When on holiday, these 'railway children' spent much time in the signal box. One swelteringly hot day, they took charge of it while the signalman went for a swim in the big water tank.

Normally, the toilet at a signal box was a tin shack a few yards from the box. At Blea Moor, an Elsan toilet stands in a compartment at the top of the signal box steps. It is related that a pipe-smoking signalman, while on the toilet, lit his pipe and dropped the match between his legs into the pan. Soon afterwards, he was aware that the temperature was rising quickly. He was not 'sickening for something' but had not extinguished the match, which fired the chemicals in the pan.

Blea Moor Cottages

Situated over a mile from Ribblehead were houses erected by the railway company for its outlying servants and their families. Letters were delivered by the Chapel-le-Dale postman, operating on foot. The Davison family, who moved to Blea Moor from Garsdale in 1933, shopped at Settle. Groceries were ordered and the goods delivered to Ribblehead station, from where they were transported to Blea Moor by local freight.

Mrs Davison, when going to the station to entrain for Settle used to recall carrying her baby in her arms. Mr Davison, a Methodist local preacher, when 'planned' at Dent would carry his bicycle through Blea Moor Tunnel, then cycle along the road to Dent. When using the tunnel, he knew the times of the trains. Not many ran on a Sunday.

Blea Moor Tunnel

It was driven for 2,629 yards at a maximum depth of some 500 ft below moor level. The stones protruding from cleared ground near the north portal do not mark the graves of navvies but indicate the area on which the Midland could legally operate.

BLEA MOOR TUNNEL. NOTE THE OLD MIDLAND RAILWAY DISTANT SIGNAL, ABOUT TO BE REPLACED IN 1997.

The men who maintained Blea Moor Tunnel found the experience weird. The place stank of sulphur. Trains passed with a hiss and flickering red light, as though Blea Moor was tenanted by dragons. There was the sound of dripping water—or silence. The north end of the tunnel was inclined to flood, and all the workers could do was to wait for the water to recede, which it did as quickly as it appeared. If the water was especially deep, part of the track might be undermined or even washed away, stopping traffic on the line.

Water, seeping in at the north end, created icicles which might be eighteen inches thick. They were knocked down by men wielding long poles—a dangerous job, for an icicle disintegrated in big lumps and those were the days before the issue of 'hard hats' to the men. The formation of icicles might be stopped using Fire Devils, or coal-fired braziers, installed on the cess side. If coal was needed for the braziers, the attendant 'caught a driver's eye' and cobs were dropped from a passing locomotive.

When the driver of a locomotive in the golden age prior to 1914 reported that water was pouring from a ventilation shaft, it was discovered that some of the 'garlands' or drainage channels were blocked. The work was carried out from the top of the shaft, on wild Blea Moor, where a jack-roll (hand-operated winch) was employed to lower a man to clean out the drains. He sat on a piece of wood fastened to the wire rope with a safety catch. The illumination was provided by a naptha lamp hanging from the seat. When he had a message that a train was due in the tunnel far below, all this workman could do was close his mouth and eyes to keep out the smoke which billowed up the shaft.

The Midland allowed a worker a white blanket coat, which did not stay white for long, and he also had thigh-length leggings. When workers deep in Blea Moor detected the approach of a train, they stopped work, such as attending to the drainage system or putting some 'packing' under sleepers, and ran for cover in one of the small manholes cut into the tunnel side. It was not unusual early this century for a member of the catering staff of an express train to hurl out unwanted food as the train passed through Blea Moor Tunnel. When an enormous catfish was discovered at the trackside by maintenance men they carted it back to their cabin, hung it up for a day or two and then destroyed it. Someone wondered why the cook had thrown it away in the first place!

In the days when a hundred steam-hauled trains a day used the Settle-Carlisle on weekdays, smoke might hang about in Blea Moor Tunnel for days on end. At times, and especially when double-headed trains were in use, visibility was reduced to zero. Tunnels were graded according to length and platelayers were paid extra for subterranean work. The figure

Continued on page 65

Above: A busy time at Settle station as passengers board and leave the morning Carlisle to Leeds train.

Below: Typical 'railway servants' cottages built by the Midland at various sites on the Settle-Carlisle route, often in very wild, out of the way places. These are at Salt Lake city near Ribblehead. Most are now privately owned.

Above: Ex-L.N.E.R. *Green Arrow* heads an express for Carlisle through the cutting just south of Blea Moor tunnel.

Below: An Inspection Special, consisting of a Class 142 unit, calls at Dent station for a brief stop during an 'out and return' tour of the line shortly after the restoration of Ribblehead viaduct. (By invitation of B.R., the authors were on board this special).

A row of porches. Midland Railway cottages were built in the style of town houses but all had substantial porches to protect the occupants from the ravages of the Pennine climate.

Ribblehead Restored. B.R. Resident Engineer, Tony Freschini and his Clerk of Works are dwarfed by the patterns of scaffolding erected for the restoration of the viaduct.

Ex-L.M.S.R. Jubilee Class No.45596 *Bahamas* starts vigorously from

Garsdale with the 'The Royal Scotsman' express, April, 1991.

Above: A green-liveried Class 40, D200 approaches Blea Moor with the morning train from Carlisle to Leeds on 6th April, 1985.

Below: Standard locomotives, Class 4, No.75014 and Class 7, No.70000, standing at Appleby station taking on water from the newly-restored water tank.

Above: Standard Class 4 tank No.80080 speeds towards Helm Tunnel on a Carlisle to Appleby local train, on a special crew-training exercise in 1993.

Below: Ex-Southern Railway *Sir Lamiel* No.777 crosses Crosby Garrett viaduct on a southbound express.

(Terminus)
A Class 156 Sprinter unit arrives at platform 6, Carlisle, on a Leeds-Carlisle train.

for Blea Moor was half a crown a week. The life-expectancy of a rail in the sulphur-ridden tunnel was about ten years—half that of a rail laid in the open. For a time, rails used in tunnels were painted to prolong their working lives.

The maintenance gang were updated with lighting equipment. Before the 1914-18 war, the naptha lamp was in use. This form of illumination was inclined to be as smoky as the trains. If a man felt devilish, he would knock over a lamp, creating a spectacular blaze. If he felt thoroughly wicked, he might throw something out of the darkness and knock over one or two lamps. The tunnel then seemed to be on fire. After the period of the naptha lamp came the Tilley, fuelled by paraffin. Eventually there was electric lighting, of a sort, attached to the tunnel wall.

A gong was installed as a warning device when an outer signal was placed in the tunnel following the installation of loop lines at Blea Moor. The gong cautioned the footplate men to look for the signal, but that gong never worked properly and was removed, the signal being placed outside the tunnel.

Strange tales are told of work being done in Blea Moor. When the track was being lifted with jacks, the approach of a train was detected by the old flagman. The ganger chuntered but the flagman insisted the arrival of a train was imminent. When the ganger looked up a second time, he saw the train approaching. There was not time to remove the jacks. For the driver of the goods train, it was—to quote him—like going over Mount Ararat. A 'slack' was operating but the men accused the driver of travelling at fifty mph. Happily for the men, the driver was persuaded this was true. Or he would have reported them.

When it was too grim for work, the maintenance gang might cower in a cave-like area called the Donkey Hole, about a quarter of a mile from the north end of the tunnel. Otherwise, a man who was moving in thick smoke kept to the prescribed course by tapping a stick on the edge of the rail.

Dent Head Viaduct

After bursting out of Blea Moor Tunnel, a train is soon running over Dent Head viaduct. No one really notices it, being entranced by the view down the dale. The viaduct comes into its own when seen from the road from near Newby Head. The structure, which is 199 yards long and 100 ft high with 10 arches is seen in the foreground of a satisfying view of Dentdale, with the slaty Howgill Fells in the distance.

The road passes through one of the arches of the viaduct. Notice, if you are a traveller by road, the single span, parapetless bridge of the type which was common in the packhorse days. It provides a splendid contrast with the railway structure.

Dent Head signal box, of which there is no trace now, the box being closed and removed in 1965, was small, approached by a field path. The box had an eight-lever tumbler frame.

A SMALL ACCESS BRIDGE

Arten Gill Viaduct

Arten Gill is a steep-sided, water-carved valley in the upper valley of the Dee. It is spanned by a 220 yard long, 11-arch structure, which has a maximum height of 117 ft. Everything about Arten Gill viaduct is impressive. The piers rest on bedrock and reaching it involved several shafts being dug to a depth of over 50 ft. The viaduct was arched with stone, not brick. The structure makes a gentle curve. It has, quite rightly, been designated as an ancient monument.

The gill is like a wind-tunnel when there are westerly gales. At times, water in the beck is blown back on itself. Arten Gill, before the coming of the railway, had a 60 ft waterfall. The gill was previously the setting for large-scale quarrying of a dark limestone which, when polished, showed up fossils in white relief. It was marketed as Dent Marble and found favour for decorative work, especially fireplaces. Some of this 'marble' went into the piers of the viaduct—piers 15 ft thick at the base tapering to six and a-half feet—and also, as fireplaces, into the station buildings of the Settle-Carlisle.

In pre-railway days, Arten Gill was dominated by the 'marble works'. Two mills, High and Low, were dedicated to cutting and polishing the pieces taken from local beds. A waterwheel with a diameter of 60 ft was enclosed in a two-storey building and provided power for these processes. In 1835, William George Armstrong and his wife Margaret, from Newcastle, ventured into the Gill. The Armstrongs were on their honeymoon. He was also finding time to indulge his sporting love, which was angling. The brown trout of the Dales rivers proved lively prey.

Entering the gill, young Armstrong saw with an engineer's eyes the workings of the machines used for cutting 'marble' and he calculated that the set-up, though ingenious, was wasteful, using only about a twentieth of the available power of the beck. Hydraulic power was the thing, and back home he worked on his ideas. Thus began a story of industrial success which led to the establishment of the great Armstrong engineering works on Tyneside.

Arten Gill viaduct used to be notable in frosty weather for having a surface which lifted. Flagmen were on duty to try to keep the speed of the traffic down to about 15 miles per hour. The driver of a steam locomotive compared the sensation of crossing Arten Gill on a frosty morning with travelling over a corrugated roof.

Dent Station

Dent, a 'small' type of station, occupies a ledge six hundred feet (1 in 4) above the main dale. The local watercourse is called Monkey Beck. Dent was brought into Settle-Carlisle service in 1877. Even more conspicuous than the main station is the Stationmaster's house, at a slightly higher elevation than the main station building.

Midland deference to the elevation and Pennine weather led to it having its walls slated on three sides and to the installation of double windows—two windows, side by side—representing an early form of double glazing. A former Stationmaster waited until there was a frosty spell before spraying the house with water from a hose pipe. The water froze, sealing the cracks and cutting down draughts. At Dent, the main buildings and the Stationmster's House are in private hands. The bridge across the tracks accommodates the old 'coal road', leading to bell-pit like workings for coal in the Yoredale series of rocks. Notice that the waiting shelter on the 'up' line is built into the hillside.

Dent was closed down for goods in October, 1964. Passenger facilites, removed in 1970, were subsequently restored. Today the station is well-endowed with Midland furniture, including diagonal platform fencing and a passenger gate of the V-trap design. The oldest folk recall when the siding was in use, dealing with cattle and also dry goods. Calves, swaddled in sacking, were sent by passenger train to Leeds. Two coal agents used the weighbridge. The last carters, Bill Moorby and David Raw, raced each other up the hill because he who arrived first had the lucrative job of collecting any parcels which had arrived by rail for delivery in the dale.

The carts, empty for the hill climb, full of coal on the way down, were not easy to control. The horse had to be experienced in order to keep its hooves on the road. With their brakes partly applied, a cart squeaked all the way down to the dale. Eventually, coal for Dent arrived via Sedbergh station. At Dent, R H Sanderson began to operate a motor lorry. His first load, baled hay, was so loose he had to borrow every rope at the station to tie it down.

The signal box installed in 1891 was made of wood with a 20 lever tumbler frame. After a blizzard, the signals at Dent usually had to be cut out of the snow. The 'distant' was so badly affected after the 1947 storm that authority gave Dent an inner-distant. When a driver saw this was 'off' he could put on steam to get through snowbound Dent cutting. The box closed in 1981 and was eventually 'put to the torch'.

Signalmen told of days when electricity was stored in batteries, the first such being glass jars with chemical additions. Later, dry batteries were in use. During the 1939-45 war, when signalmen were supposed to wear tin hats, windows were covered with cellophane and an air raid shelter was established in the box. When at times of maximum alert, traffic on the line was stopped, one signalman "turned my lamp down, lay down in the box, and dreamed I was rabbiting in a local wood." Two bombs fell on nearby Hollow Mill Pasture.

Unofficial visits to signal boxes were discouraged, yet Bishop Treacy of Wakefield was always welcome. On his first visits, he wore collar and tie. When his identity as a Bishop became known to the railwaymen, who were inclined to swear a lot, they curbed their language. He sighed and said that he enjoyed his talks with the men.

Dent was vulnerable to snow and lines of upreared railway sleepers were set up as a barrier. This station was made the base for snow-clearing teams. A stone billet near the signal box provided a resting place for men engaged in snow-cutting and ploughing.

Rise Hill Tunnel

Lying to the north of Dent station, this tunnel was cut for 1,213 yards through unstable rock. It was necessary to use iron ribs tied with rods for support. Two air shafts ventilate the tunnel. Access to Rise Hill was not easy and involved making a track from the Coal Road. Much of the debris from the tunnel, which had been heaped up, was used for further road-making when the area was planted with conifer trees. These now hide the construction scars.

Garsdale Troughs

Having water available for thirsty locomotives was a vital necessity. The high Pennine rainfall ensured there was water in plenty. Water-cranes were installed where possible. To the south of Garsdale station, where there is a long, straight stretch of track, water-troughs with a length of 1,670 ft, and a capacity of between 5,000 and 6,000 gallons, were fitted. These troughs, installed in 1907 at a cost of £4,396, were long since removed. In their day they were the highest in the land, being designed to fill up in about ten minutes under normal circumstances.

Nearly all the expresses picked up water at Garsdale, though the troughs were 'chancy', being frozen over in winter, dry in summer and clogged with fallen leaves in autumn. The Garsdale gang spent much time in winter picking ice from between trough and rail, which lessened the risk of a train leaving the tracks, the men being provided with clogs because the area was generally slippery.

At one time, the water was heated by a steam pipe from a boiler in a tank house, the steam passing through copper pipes. A man on night duty stoked up the fire, using for some of the time coal which had been washed from the tenders of passing trains. Over fifty men were involved in the installation of a dam. A moorland beck was diverted. Cement for the dam was conveyed across the moor on a light railway.

On completion of the dam, some 'top brass' arrived and the stream was allowed to follow its old course. The man in charge of the dam, anxious to save the railway company money, had not used enough cement in the mixture. The dam leaked like a cylinder and the work had to be done again.

In the 1950s, the heavy troughs were removed for maintenance. A few years later they were taken up and sent for scrap.

Garsdale Station

Garsdale, the only true junction station on the Settle-Carlisle, is remote from large settlements and gives the impression of being an outpost, set in a scenically outstanding area, the main view taking in Wild Boar Fell and Mallerstang Edge. The Midland had planned to build an engine shed for a large number of locomotives, with no less than 30 'railway servants' cottages'. These ambitious plans were modified and Garsdale became important at the point where pilot engines were removed from double-headed trains which were then sent back to Carlisle or Hellifield.

Grandly known as Hawes Junction when it was opened in 1876s, and having an island platform, it became Hawes Junction and Garsdale, simplified to Garsdale in 1932. The station lost its junction status with the closure of the Wensleydale line down to Redmire in 1959. An engine shed used by NER engines working services to Hawes was burnt down in 1917, rebuilt, and closed for good in 1939. Garsdale had extensive cattle docks. The famous turntable, where once an engine at the mercy of the wind was whipped round and round, leading to the fitting of a stockade made of sleepers, was removed and taken to the Keighley and Worth Valley line.

Garsdale still welcomes trains and the signal box on the 'down' platform remains. The present box was brought into use in 1910, when signal boxes at North Junction and South Junction were taken out of service. With an increased work load, it was built especially large, having a length of thirty feet and containing a 40 lever tappet frame. The box went out of primary use in 1983 but is kept operational and comes into its own on special occasions.

Garsdale was for many years a social centre for a wide area of sparsely populated dale country. The Midland built sixteen company houses, where large families were the norm and Garsdale Head had a generous scattering of small farms. But shopping facilities were sparse, limited to a small shop near the station. The LMS compensated for this paucity of shopping facilities by granting a free pass each week to the wives of railwaymen so that they might visit local markets—Hawes (six miles) or Settle (twenty miles).

Dances, domino and whist drives, potato pie suppers and concerts, held in the Tank House from about 1918, were attended by railway and farm folk. A fund-raising event to modify the Tank House yielded the sum of £25 to provide a good floor, composed of laid sleepers, over which were fitted tongued and grooved boards. It was reported to be like a skating rink at times. The money raised also covered the cost of a gramophone, a piano, lamps and other items.

The place was reported to be cheerfully decorated. A piano and accordion usually provided the music for 'sixpenny hops', but on special occasions there was a small band and there might be over a hundred people packed into the Tank House and the adjacent 'supper room; which was an old railway carriage, fitted with stove and boiler, with seating and tables for the hungry or exhausted patrons. The only drink available was tea. Food was on the Jacob's Join principal whereby each person attending contributed to the common store of eatables. Several concerts, with local artistes, were held to enliven the long Garsdale winter.

A visitor to Garsdale in 1938 noted that if a rail-user had an honest face he or she might go into the waiting room to borrow a book from a unique little library, the nucleus being a stock of 150 books given by two elderly ladies from Wensleydale who often used the station. The Stationmaster became chief librarian. Books were let out free of charge to the railway staff. At one time, the 'down' platform was used as a chapel. In 1938, it still had the organ and "a few moth 'eaten hymn books".

Garsdale's famous Tank House was demolished in 1971.

Moorcock Viaduct

The viaduct which was first named Dandry Mire and is now the Moorcock cuts across the head of Garsdale with considerable visual impact. The viaduct in its austere setting is beloved of railway photographers, who can portray the 'steam-specials' in spacious surroundings, filling half the photographic frame with sky and half the sky with engine smoke.

The name Moorcock relates to the hostelry at the junction between the Hawes-Sedbergh highway and the road heading northwards to Kirkby Stephen. The hostelry, in turn, was named after the red grouse, which is well-suited to the *calluna* moors of this area. Temperance Hotel was the grand name give to No.13 Railway Cottages at Garsdale, where Mr and Mrs Reuben Alton provided accommodation for visitors, mainly commercial travellers.

At Dandry Mire, an embankment was planned and tipping activity went on for a considerable time. The hope was to create solid ground but the effect was simply a bulging of the sides of the mire. In 1871, a viaduct was proposed. The mire was drained when a trench was cut through deep peat. A solid foundation was found for the piers of the viaduct, which has a length of 227 yards, with 12 arches. The fourth and eighth piers were made more substantial than the others.

Chapel and Road Bridge

A prominent feature of the view from the train as it leaves Garsdale is 't'Junction chapel', of Methodist persuasion, standing in solitary splendour beside the Hawes-Sedbergh road, almost in the shadow of a 39 ft 6 in skew arch, constructed in 1872. Notice the arch-relieved wing walls. Chapel and bridge have grown up together. Each became operational in 1876. It is believed that railway navvies were among those who helped to build the place of worship.

Mount Zion chapel, to use its full name, consists literally of one room with a steep-pitched roof and a lile porch. It was used in a television documentary about rural Methodism, a film which featured Herbert Silverwood, an evangelist who had been 'packing 'em in' at dales chapels for many years. Though small, the chapel has accommodated over 100 people on special occasions. Others have had to spend the afternoon out of doors.

The foundation stone of this tiny chapel was laid by Reuben Alton, whose family came to this district from Leeds. (Reuben was buried in another small local chapel, that at Garsdale Smithy).

Moorcock Cottages

Six railway servants' cottages, in the now familiar Midland style, have been given the added protection of slates attached to the gable end and front of the first dwelling. A wash-house across the yard was used by some families as a bathhouse.

In times past, water was carried for some 200 yards from a spring under the fourth arch of the viaduct. In the absence of electricity, paraffin lamps were in use after dark and residents went to bed by candlelight. The man at the end house was paid at the rate of half a crown each for emptying the earth closets. He wheeled the stuff across the road in a barrow and dumped it in the field for the farmer to spread as manure.

Moorcock Inn

The solitary building, which is situated 11 miles from Kirkby Stephen, 10 miles from Sedbergh and five miles from Hawes, is of such strategic importance it is marked on most maps of England. Little is known of its history. Kit Calvert, the sage of upper Wensleydale, had heard that, towards the end of the 18th century and in the early part of the 19th century, this was one of two public houses which sheltered Scottish drovers as they travelled southwards with cattle or sheep. They came up Mallerstang or over Nine Standards Rigg from Stainmore, and after a sojourn at the Moorcock continued up the old road to Newby Head and Gearstones.

In 1841, the name of the hostelry was Guide Post Inn. An advertisement states that "by the desire of several of the principal Graziers and Stock-keepers in Craven etc.", a fair for the buying and selling of cattle and sheep would be held behind the Inn on 9th July. The advertisement added that the inn stood on the road between Hawes, Sedbergh and Kirkby Stephen "and there is a driving road from thence over the moors by Newby Head to Settle, Ingleton and Skipton, etc., on which there are no Toll Bars."

Kit recalled a tragic incident on December 24, 1910, when they carried into the Moorcock ten disfigured bodies of those who died in the wreck of the Scots express. The bodies were kept here until identified and an inquest had taken place. Years ago, the Lunesdale Foxhounds met at the Moorcock and supporters had a hunt ball in tiny Lunds School. In the 1970s, the inn was gutted by fire. It was to rise, pheonix-like, from the ashes, the old burnt roof timbers, some four inches thick, being sawed down to the good wood and, after being sanded, used as the pitchpine bar top of the new premises.

Moorcock Tunnel

This tunnel, which is comparatively short, at 98 yards, was cut through boulder clay, a geological mush related to the close of the Ice Age. It proved to be most troublesome to the Midland engineers who one day might spoon it from its bed and soon afterwards, following dry weather, found it had set as hard as concrete. Moorcock Tunnel has a slight curve. Side walls, wings and arch are of stone.

Lunds Viaduct

A five-arch, stone viaduct with a length of 193 yards and maximum height of 63 ft. It was hereabouts that one of the most serious accidents to befall traffic on the Settle-Carlisle ocurred. This was on Christmas Eve, 1910, when two light engines which had banked trains up to Ais Gill, and had continued to Garsdale to turn, were waiting for a clear road back to Carlisle. Overlooking their presence, the signalman pulled off the signals for a St Pancras-Glasgow express.

The drivers of the banking engines took this as clearing the line for them and consequently they set off, crossing Moorcock Viaduct, passing through the tunnel and travelling at a relatively slow pace towards Lunds. The express, which was travelling at 65 miles an hour, caught up with them on the far side of Lunds Viaduct. The gas-lit carriages broke into flames with the force of the impact. Twelve people died, several of them being interred in a (now closed) graveyard at Hawes.

In the old Midland days, some scaffolding used at Lunds was moved on bogeys to Garsdale and down the Hawes branch. A flagman stationed down the line cautioned trains about this special traffic. The driver of a goods train who failed to see the flagman startled the men with the bogeys when it suddenly appeared about half a mile away. The men jumped to one side before the train, braking fiercely, collided with the bogeys. Scaffolding was spread all over the track. The driver of the goods train was suspended from work for a short time for his lack of attention.

Shotlock Hill Tunnel

Prominent when seen from the road but a modest affair, a mere 98 yards long.

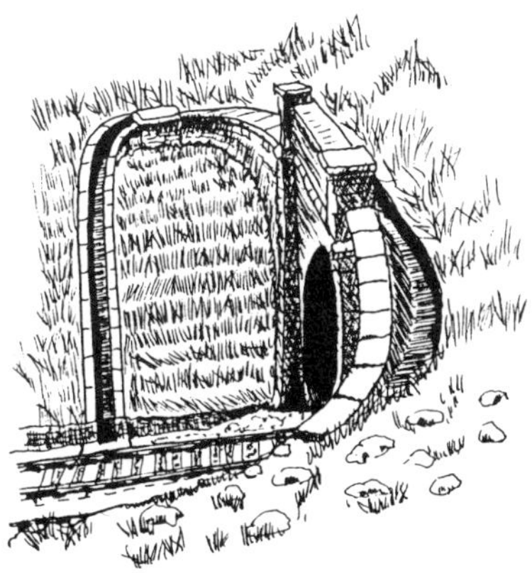

SURFACE WATER DRAINAGE
AT SHOTLOCK TUNNEL

Grisedale Crossing

A plate-girder footbridge is a novel feature on the Settle-Carlisle. It replaced the original bridge, of timber, which was built in 1886. A footpath leads to the bridge, which is a good place to stand if photographs are required of special trains.

Grisedale ('valley of pigs') is out of sight of the footbridge, being usually approached on a road from the head of Garsdale. It became well-known to viewers of Yorkshire Television as 'the dale that died'. It is still very much alive.

Ais Gill

The highest point of the Settle-Carlisle (1,169 ft) is at Aisgill, the precise spot being marked by large nameboards. Those who lived at Aisgill claimed that many a time they had snow when none fell at Garsdale. Memories linger on about the Great Snow of 1947, when the Settle-Carlisle was blocked for weeks on end, though trains continued to run from Hawes to Garsdale and food for the people was piled upon the locomotive. Snowploughs were decked with fodder for starving animals. The RAF from Dishforth, using Dakotas, delivered bales of hay by air. One pilot was so precise in his haydrop that a bale went through a farmhouse roof.

The signal box which stood here until recent times was a replacement in 1890 of the original structure. The box, with its 16 lever tumbler frame, closed in 1981 and was moved to Derbyshire to stand beside a preserved railway. In its Ais Gill setting, there was a wooden walkway from the box to the embankment.

Westbound travellers by road cross the old Westmorland/North Riding boundary (which is now on the border between Cumbria and North Yorkshire). A sign indicates the Yorkshire Dales National Park. Railway cottages (which lack the usual small dormers, having a continuous roofline) stood in Old Westmorland, the signal box of blessed memory being in Yorkshire.

A waterfall viewed from the eastern side of the train is where Hell Gill beck, a nursery stretch of the Eden, makes a spectacular leap on its way into Mallerstang. (Hell, the name of a ravine, is derived from *hella,* a Norse word for cave. The ravine is too cold and wet to hold the Devil). Where the road to Kirkby Stephen crosses the line there was a railway accident with affinities to that at Lunds.

It occurred in September, 1913, when two sleeping car expresses were climbing to Ais Gill. They had left Carlisle with a quarter of an hour interval. The first express was heavy enough to warrant being double-headed but left Carlisle without a pilot. Each locomotive had been supplied with inferior coal, which led to problems on the climb. The first train stalled when it had almost reached the summit.

The crew of the second train, concentrating on coaxing their locomotive on the ascent, went through several adverse signals. The second train plunged into the rear of the first, with eighteen fatilities. The grave of the victims is in Kirkby Stephen cemetery, on the north side of the town. The impressive headstone is now almost covered with moss and lichen.

A lady who went as a bride to Ais Gill in 1927, her husband being a signalman, had to pay a penny a year to the landowner for every stoop she erected to support her washing line. One wash-day, in this moorland setting, she once almost stood on the nest of a pair of lapwings.

Ais Gill Viaduct

This four-arch structure, with a length of 87 yards, has four stone-built spans and a maximum height of 75 ft. The gill itself is little-known because no public right of way exists. It is indeed a spectacular notch, with a lively beck and a profusion and variety of ferns.

Mallerstang

Mallerstang is an impressive trough between Wild Boar Fell and Mallerstang Edge. Many good walkers enjoy the experience of walking between the railway stations of Garsdale and Kirkby Stephen along one side or other of the valley, in either case revelling in the fine-weather views. In Mallerstang itself, a visitor observes fellsides which sweep upwards for 2,000 ft or more. When a fierce wind blows, becks may be blown back on themselves as fine vapour, giving the impression of smoke.

The Settle-Carlisle keeps high above the valley, offering the best views of the valley, with its string of farms, its pattern of drystone walls, a little church (restored by Lady Anne Clifford) and the remains of a castle named Pendragon, the home ('they' say) of Uther Pendragon, who was the father of Arthur of Round Table fame. Pendragon's ancient masonry has now been consolidated. It is a most picturesque ruin.

The stretch of line between Garsdale and Kirkby Stephen, a distance of 9¾ miles, is the longest without a station. A proposal to build a passenger station in Mallerstang, opposite Outhgill, foundered when the necessary local money was not available to create the road approach. The signal box, with attendant sidings, was closed in 1969. For a time platelayers took over the box. One day, when they left an especially large fire, the box burnt down.

Mallerstang box had a lonely situation. On especially dark nights, the signalman who left his bike in the churchyard at Outhgill before climbing the hillside to the box could not always find the stiles. He had to clamber over the walls. Sometimes, he waited until a train was passing before fixing his position and planning the next stage of the walk.

There was no water supply in the box, the water being taken from a small stream at the lineside, some way off. A new signalman who collected water in this way was not keen to drink it when a colleague said he had seen a dead horse lying in the beck higher up the fell. Charlie Metcalfe, a signalman at Mallerstang, bred fell ponies in his spare time.

Bridges with wooden staging gave the Mallerstang farmers passage from their farms to the upland pastures. A ganger who was astonished at the number of sheep he picked up dead on the line near one such bridge kept watch, for the farmer was seeking compensation from the railway company. The ganger's patience was rewarded when the farmer arrived at the bridge with a dead sheep, lifted a loose board on a bridge and dropped the animal on to the line.

In 1931, snow lay so deep at Mallerstang it extended to the height of the signal. About this time, the Settle-Carlisle was issued with a new all-steel snow plough which fitted on the front buffer beam of a locomotive, the plough replacing the large wooden combined ploughs and accommodation vans for the attendants. The old plough-vans held six shovels, painted red, and ramps for attending to derailed vans.

Down Mallerstang was the Golden Culvert, taking water from Wild Boar Fell. The reference to gold was a reflection of the high cost of its construction and the fact it was not cheap to maintain. When trees were washed into it, partly blocking the flow of water, it was essential to clear the obstruction quickly. It was known for the men to swim for their lives when the water flow was resumed.

Birkett Tunnel

This 424 yard long tunnel has a deep cutting to the south and is crossed by a road from Pendragon to the A 683. Hereabouts is the Great Pennine Fault where, as Derek Cross wrote, "the limestones and millstone grits are left behind, and the warm, red earths of the Eden Valley start." Miners involved in Birkett Tunnel encountered shale, mountain limestone, magnesium limestone, slate, grit, iron, even a coal seam and lead ore. The hand method of drilling was greatly improved on through the use of the Burleigh rock drill, which bit into rock at the rate of one foot every five minutes. Birkett Tunnel was constructed with a brick arch ring throughout.

The driver of a steam locomotive, emerging from the north end of Birkett tunnel, looked out for what he called a 'black burr' or bar—evidence that the Helm Wind was blowing. It was most active in the vicinity of High Cup Nick, opposite Appleby, but its effects were felt right along the eastern fells as far as Mallerstang. The Wind was known to blow lumps of coal off the fireman's shovel, and though there was a strong door on a Class 5, the Helm would waft it open. It was customary to place a coal hammer against the door to restrain it.

Tozer, a worker in Birkett Tunnel, was so named because, while cleaning the rails, and often revealing the red lead painted on them when they were new, he deciphered the maker's name—Peach and Tozer of Workington.

Kirkby Stephen Station

This station, which has the same generous specifications as Settle and Appleby, was equipped with a large goods shed and cattle dock. After many years of operation, serving farmers and businessmen over a wide area, the goods service ended in 1964 and the yard is now used by Sam Ostle & Sons, who are well-known road hauliers.

Kirkby Stephen (West) is perched on a hill, some two miles from the market town after which it is named. Such a remote spot was necessary of course to establish a good working gradient at Aisgill, the Settle-Carlisle highspot. (Much closer to the town was the North Eastern Railway's system between Darlington and Tebay). The railway bridges the Kendal-Brough road. On the high side of the bridge are Midland Cottages, with Midland Terrace and the Stationmaster's House below the bridge.

When Brough Hill Horse Fair was held near Warcop, horses and ponies entrained at Kirkby Stephen, creating much excitement, for many of them were unbroken, bewildered and beaten at will by anyone with a stick or whip. The permanent way men at Kirkby Stephen were loaned to the Traffic Department to assist with loading the animals into cattle trucks and horse boxes.

When permanent way men had repaired to the Croglin to limber up for the coming ordeal with horses, George Buck (whose turn it was to pay for a round of pints) was relieved when he heard the distant *clip, clop* of 400 animals belting up the road. Now was the hour when he could save some money. He yelled: "Hosses is coming!" before dashing out of the inn.

Smardale Viaduct

Smardale is superb when viewed from ground level. With a length of 237 yards and 14 lofty arches, the highest at 131 ft, Smardale drapes itself over the valley of the Scandal Beck. The viaduct was constructed of stone taken from a quarry about a mile upstream. In the absence of a local deposit of sand for mortar, the contractor used burnt clay until sand was brought in along the NER.

Smardale is now a reserve, rich in plant life including orchids and, in summer, being a-flutter with Scotch Argus butterflies. The old trackbed of the NER line between Tebay and Kirkby Stephen is now a footpath, the most exciting stretch being where it crosses the restored old Smardale viaduct.

Crosby Garrett Tunnel

A short tunnel (181 yards), it cut through a local fell, the tunnellers encountering gritstone, limestone and flint. The tunnel was provided with stone side walls and faces, the arch being of brick.

Crosby Garrett Viaduct

With a length of 110 yards, this graceful limestone viaduct attains a maximum height of 55 ft and offers a splendid view of the village, a notable building being the church, standing on a green mound.

Crosby Garrett Station

Built in a cutting, this attractive Midland station is no more, though the Stationmaster's house survives, in private hands. The platforms were among the longest on the Midland system. Notice the indentations left by waiting rooms which were demolished.

When the Express Dairy opened a plant at Appleby, a special milk train from Hawes called at Crosby Garrett, and the staff became adroit at moving seventeen gallon kits. In the 1930s, most farmers arriving with milk at Crosby Garrett had horses and traps. In its heyday, Crosby Garrett had a sizable goods shed, a cattle dock and a goodly range of platform structures, now all gone.

Telegrams which were transmitted to the signal box were delivered by any lads who might be playing nearby. One lad, riding a bike, made a round trip of about eight miles and was paid 1s.6d for his pains.

Grizeburn Viaduct

With seven limestone arches striding for 142 yards over Potts Beck (or Helm Beck, as it was known to the Midland men), and the tallest pier having a height of 74 ft, this viaduct marks the halfway point of the Settle-Carlisle railway. The abutments, wings, piers and parapets are of stone, with red sandstone facings and brick arches.

Griseburn Ballast Sidings

Griseburn, remote and quiet, had a signal box at the old ballast quarry, which was in use from the late 1880s until 1914-18, then closed until 1939. When the sidings closed, the signal continued to be used as a block post, ceasing to operate in 1981.

During the Great Snow of 1947, one of the Griseburn signalmen who was lodging at Asby, about three miles away, did not heed the words of his landlady, that if he got to work that night he would never get back because of heavy snow. He struggled to work, for the two to ten shift, and settled down to work, but no traffic came. When he looked out of the box at 10pm, he discovered the cutting was overblown.

Fortunately, he had plenty of food in his bag, for the landlady killed a pig for domestic use and also had her own flock of hens. The signalman was in the box for three days, using up coal from a big pile in the corner and water from three large containers. The two other signalman did not get to work, but eventually he discovered to his annoyance they had been paid for the time they were absent.

EX-M.R. KIRTLEY 0-6-0 GOODS LOCOMOTIVE,
WITH ORIGINS FROM 1863.

Ormside Station

Ormside station, set in a quiet countryside, some distance from the village, was constructed of contrasting light and dark stonework. Passenger trains ceased to call in 1952. The signal box closed in 1960.

Frank Ridding, signalman at Ormside, was also a cobbler who got an allocation of leather during the 1939-45 war. Drivers of steam trains would sling off a pair of shoes as they were passing Ormside box. A note gave their expected time of repair. Frank usually had the work done in time, charging 12s.6d for soling and heeling.

Ormside Viaduct

The Settle-Carlisle crosses the Eden for the first time at Ormside, where one of the 90 ft piers is actually standing in water. Ormside is stone-built, except the arches, which are lined with bricks.

Appleby Station

'Appleby' is displayed in whitened stones on the embankment above the 'up' platform. Of the large type, this station was built of brick, dressed with stone, being until recent times the only station on the line with a passenger footbridge. It is a stopping place for 'steam specials' having watering facilities. A plaque on the main station building is a memorial to Bishop Treacy, railway photographer extraordinary, who collapsed and died here on a special 'steam' day.

Half a mile south of Appleby station, Express Dairy Company of London created in 1931 an Appleby plant from which local milk was transported daily to the Capital in special 3,000 gallon tanker wagons lined with glass. Originally, they were attached to the 3.26pm train from Appleby. As farmers in the district became more confident about the milk scheme, production on the farms rose and a special train was arranged which took six tanker-wagons northwards to Carlisle, where they were attached to a train which also served Nestles.

The combined load was then conveyed speedily southwards, to the Express plant at Cricklewood, so that milk drawn from the cows of Edendale one day was, early on the following day, in bottles adorning the doorsteps or retail shops of London. At the peak, Express Dairy was sending away 27 tanks of milk a day.

Appleby was one of the first places from which prize cattle were sent away in boxes, which were called 'prize cattle wagons' but were, in truth, just horse boxes. The cows were transported over a wide area. When a horse box was being used for horses—and the capacity was three—one end was modified to provide a simple lodging for the attendant, who was thus able to sleep if travelling overnight.

Every railwayman was proficient at herding cattle. At about 7.15am, a gang assembling at Appleby to join the 7.40am passenger train included some experienced cattlemen, whose farming experience came in useful when one small animal in a consignment of animals being received by the Winter Brothers began to calve. It was a breech birth. Bill Balmer doffed his billycock hat, kytle, waistcoat and shirt and assisted. He got the leg doubled back and the head eased out. The calf was born on the platform. Bill washed himself down in the cattle trough, dried off in the porter's room—and caught the train!

Long Marton Viaduct

The viaduct crosses Troutbeck and has five lofty spans and a length of 108 yards. Red sandstone for the structure came from a quarry in Dufton Gill, two miles away. The abutments, piers and parapets are of stone. The arches are lined with brick.

Long Marton Station

The medium size of building was selected. A brick structure was set off with the use of red sandstone for quoins, plinth and window surrounds. Long Marton had a good deal of mineral traffic, including barytes from the Silverband Mine, high on Dun Fell, the barytes being conveyed by aerial ropeway. The most southerly deposits of gypsum were at Long Marton. The station was closed in 1970.

At Long Marton, washing was hung on the embankment, which was called The Batters. The top of the redundant signal box at Newbiggin was transported to Long Marton and used as a greenhouse. At Long Marton, in 1943, the rent for a railway house was 7s.6d a week, which was deducted from a man's wages. The company carried out decorations, both outside and inside, the paint used being of a chocolate colour.

Kirkby Thore

Several trains a day bring gypsum from the Drax power station to the plasterboard works at Kirkby Thore, where there are special sidings and a state-of-the-art signalbox. Gypsum has been mined locally. It has been said, tongue in cheek, that hereabouts the Settle-Carlisle runs on pit props.

In the operation, limestone from the Peak District is transferred by rail to Drax, where it is used to remove sulphur dioxide from the emission gases and thus reduces the problem of 'acid rain' throughout Europe. The end product of the Drax process is a substance known by the unwieldy name of Desulphogypsum (DSG), which can be used in the manufacture of plasterboard. The type of locomotive used on the Settle-Carlisle is a Class 60, with a Mirlees engine, producing 3,100 h.p.

Newbiggin Station

This station of the small type of building stands in a village which has a rosy tint from golden-hued freestone and red sandstone. A familiar sight at the country stations in early summer was the arrival, in special vans, of the hessian wool sheets needed for the 'clip'. A representative of Pickles would tour the farms and take orders for sheets. The wrapped wool was taken to the station by arrangement and loaded into a van.

Culgaith Station and Level Crossing

The Midland did not propose to build a station at Culgaith, so the Vicar and local landowners wrote directly to Midland headquarters at Derby, asking for one to be provided. The company agreed, but half-heartedly. Opened in 1880, several years after the line was in operation, this was not the usual substantial Derby Gothic type of station but cottage-style, with cock's comb ridge tiles and wooden platforms.

It still exists but is not used as such. Culgaith became an unstaffed halt in 1967 and was closed to passengers in 1970. A signalbox and level crossing, with adjacent small goods yard, are the important features. Goods facilities were withdrawn in 1964 but the box controls the level crossing.

Culgaith station has a rural setting, with a garden centre on one side. There is a cafe, where the food is home-made. Walls and beams are decked with objects relating to the Settle-Carlisle, which has a varied wildlife. The signalman on duty at Culgaith would not be surprised to see a fox or a hare cross the track. Rabbits scutter from under the plank-walk.

The river is fishable, to those with permits. Every other week-end, in the old days, Mr Hinchcliffe of Halifax, who was a keen angler, arrived at Culgaith Station on the last train to run on Saturday. He was conveyed to the Kings Arms at Temple Sowerby. On Monday morning, when the porter at Culgaith arrived early, he found a parcel of fish being sent to Halifax. The porter had four sixpences ready—sixpence for himself, sixpence for the guard who would take a parcel of fish to Keighley, sixpence for the North East guard who would take it down to Halifax, and sixpence for the porter who delivered it to Mr Hinchcliffe's home.

In the old days, nine farmers sent milk away daily. A charge of 1s.4d was made for transporting a large churn of milk to Carlisle and on to Newcastle. Included in the charge was the return of the empty churn. One farmer who took five big churns daily left them on a barrow and paid a local man 2s to put them on the train for him. This enabled the farmer to make a prompt return to his holding.

Culgaith Tunnel

With a length of 661 yards, the tunnel was driven through red marl and was provided with brick side walls, invert and arch having stone faces. A single, 74 ft deep shaft ventilates the tunnel.

From Culgaith, one might see through the tunnel. A stock joke locally is about a new porter who was standing with a man at the crossing gates as a train approached. The porter, who was in a daft frame of mind, remarked: "That train has a good driver, sir. He's gone straight through the hole without any difficulty." The man looked incredulous and said: "I didn't know the driver had to steer."

Waste Bank Tunnel

Another short tunnel, to the north of Culgaith. In March, 1930, two trains collided, a passenger train running into one carrying ballast. The rotary block was indirectly the cause of this accident. The intervening Culgaith tunnel stopped an intermediate flagman from giving a visual signal that the 'down slow' had left Appleby. The Culgaith signalman, wishing to give the ballast train a good margin, arranged with the attendant flagman that he would wag the 'up' distant signal, which was between the two tunnels.

Langwathby signalled an 'up' freight on line, so there was no chance of wagging the distant. The fireman on the passenger train, who was driving at the time, passed the 'down' starter at danger. The guard, who was doing his written work, assumed the signal had come off. Meanwhile, in Culgaith tunnel there was no secondary flagman and no fog signal on the line. If Joe Hogarth had not raised the alarm, the passenger train would have killed two maintenance gangs, nos 201 and 202.

The northbound train bursts out of Waste Bank Tunnel and treats passengers to a view of Edenvale at its most sensuous. The ground slips away to huge level fields abutting the Eamont, which gives the Eden a transfusion of cold, clear Lakeland water at a place called appropriately Watersmeet. In winter, before the land is turned 'brown side up' by the ploughs, this is an area where huge flocks of greylag geese are found. Some are native born and others come from Iceland, having crossed five hundred miles of open water to a British landfall.

Langwathby Station

An imaginative writer reeled off the names of some of the Edenvale villages—Langwathby, Little Salkeld, Lazonby—and commented they roll off the tongue like a Gregorian chant. At Langwathby, rosy-red in sunshine from the local sandstone, is a station which falls in the 'medium' category. The stationmaster's house was built near the Alston road, at the entrance to the station.

Langwathby was closed to passengers in 1970 after being unstaffed since 1967. Goods traffic had ceased in 1964. It was re-opened and has received much attention. Here there is a 'feel good' factor, especially in the main building, where a cafe was opened with the evocative name of *Brief Encounter,* though it is far north of Carnforth, where outdoor scenes for a film of that name were shot.

Langwathby, a large village with open green spaces, used its station a good deal during old-time harvests, when a large quantity of potatoes were consigned to Lancashire towns, the Co-op being the best customers. Local lads would visit the station in the evening to pick up some of the 'taties' which had spilled during the loading of low wagons and roast them at the waiting room fire.

Little Salkeld

Edenvale had some eccentric landowners. A choleric man at Little Salkeld waylaid the length ganger as he drove in pegs to indicate the positions for permanent steel boundary posts. The landowner kicked out all the pegs, tossing them

LONG MEG AND HER DAUGHTERS

away. On the occasion of a family wedding, this landowner entertained some guests by giving joy-rides on Little Salkeld platform, using the four-wheeler truck.

Sidings, rail connections and signal box appeared from 1896, when Long Meg Plaster and Mineral Co., Ltd., had workings in the area. The box seen today came into use in 1955 and was active until 1963. Long Meg mine was the only gypsum mine adjacent to the Settle-Carlisle line to have a ghost. The mysterious sounds were doubtless natural.

The farmer at Long Meg Farm, near one of the most impressive prehistoric stone circles in the land, heard sounds which would be mysterious to strangers but, to him, indicated a change of shift at the mine, some distance away.

Eden Lacy Viaduct

This 137 yard long viaduct was fashioned from red sandstone between 1871 and 1875. No less than four of the six piers are set in the bed of the Eden. The alternative name for the viaduct is Long Meg, originally used by the engineer's department. Long Meg mine is not far away.

Lazonby Sand Hole

The railway owned this source of good sand situated south of Lazonby Tunnel. Sand taken from the pits was transported to motive power depots for use on locomotives, which fed dry sand directly on to the rails to obtain a grip in greasy conditions or when the gradient was especially steep.

At first, sand was despatched only to Midland loco depots, but during the 1914-18 war the staff at the Sand Hole was increased from a basic two men to a staff capable of supplying depots in other regions. With less care being taken, there were occasional complaints by locomotive superintendents, including (in 1946) a New Year's Card in which it was hoped future supplies of sand would be free of sods, stones, soil, clay and other foreign objects. The sender of the card attached it to a cocoa tin in which were samples of the aforementioned objects.

A steam crane was introduced to speed up delivery. The Sand Hole was in use until the summer of 1963, when the siding was removed and the Hole itself, now too deep for economical use, ceased to be used.

Lazonby and Kirkoswald

The villages are on different banks of the Eden, but the station is most definitely at Lazonby, where the northbound traveller finds him/herself in a 99 yard long tunnel. It was originally planned to have a cutting, but engineers tend to err on the side of safety. The tunnel was cut and this brief gloomy period increases the pleasure of suddenly arriving in a glorious redstone village, not much changed over the years, with the church and an inn called the Midland situated not far from the station. A bakery has bought much of the land which was formerly owned by the railway.

A medium-sized station, Lazonby became an unstaffed halt in 1967 and was closed to passengers in 1970, to be re-opened when new life came back to the system. The adjacent bridge was built entirely of stone, each span being of 25 ft. The parapet on the western side was augmented by iron railings so that a passenger leaving the coach of a train which was too long to fit in the platform would not step over the parapet

TYPICAL MIDLAND GOODS SHED AND SIGNAL

and plunge on to the road below.

The signal box, installed in 1895, closed in 1969. Lazonby goods yard handled a good deal of timber which Greens, the wood merchants, acquired from local forests. The cattle dock, so named, was employed to deal with vast numbers of sheep in autumn. Goods facilities had been lost five years earlier.

With its sandy soil, Lazonby gained the distinction of being able to grow bigger carrots than any other place along the Settle-Carlisle line. The village's sylvan setting appealed to 'toffs' from Bradford and Leeds who, especially when salmon were running, stayed at the Brackenbank Hotel, using it as their base for fishing exursions. Ghillies took them out on the river by boat. An angler was allowed to keep one salmon but any others caught were despatched to Edwards and Walden of London.

Lazonby, being not too far from Carlisle, had a local commuter trade with Carlisle. A bank manager caught an early train and while waiting for it warmed himself at the big stove in the booking office. Schoolchildren took the first train for Carlisle to attend school.

Most of the objects and produce needed by a such a rural community arrived by train. The 'coal road' was always busy, having three dealers based upon it. The dealers received coal supplies in bulk and employed men to bag it for distribution, though farmers with horses and carts arrived to collect coal, usually 'Carlton Hards', in large cobs, which was loaded by hand and cost 15s a cartload. A horse had to negotiate a steep hill in Lazonby, so the cart must not be overladen. When using the station weighing machine, the cart was drawn on to it and the shafts propped so that "you weren't weighing t'hoss as well".

Lazonby has long been a major centre for farm stock, especially sheep. When dealers visited the Scottish sales, up to four special trains holding sheep were dealt with at Lazonby each day. The main dealers, who represented farmers round about, brought the railway so much revenue they had a special concession. The Scotch express was stopped for them at 4.30am, so they might make an early start for St Boswells.

Johnny Graham, who headed the reception committee for sheep bought at the Scottish sales, worked wonders in accommodating a large number of wagons in the limited space of the Lazonby cattle dock, which held nine or ten wagons at a time. Johnny was constantly moving a train, whipping the empties out and bringing in the full ones. He contrived, not always successfully, to count the sheep affected by these rapid movements.

Lazonby sheep sales are still famous. In the days before motor transport for stock, up to 55 wagons were dealt with by the Lazonby railway staff who, to quote one of them, "didn't need to be rocked to sleep that evening." Lazonby also had a lively trade in rabbits. Three men who supplied rabbits to the trade had a small wagon each and went round the country villages, several times a week, collecting rabbits which were put in crates (20 couple to the crate) and despatched to the markets of Bradford and Leeds, with a smaller quantity going to Newcastle.

During the 1939-45 war, a Carlisle driver, Bill Barnum, was stopped at Lazonby and told that his relief had just arrived. A driver presented himself. He was about to climb on to the engine when Bill restrained him. How did he know that this man, a stranger to him, was not an enemy agent? Bill told him to ride on the brake. At about the same time, a porter at Lazonby climbed on to the bogie bolsters of a train to take a closer look at what appeared to be very large torpedoes.

An Army officer intervened. The strange objects were miniature submarines destined for a hush-hush attack in Norwegian waters.

Eden Gorge

Between Lazonby and Armathwaite lies a redstone gorge festooned with trees, some of them old and enough of them belonging to the pine family to give the area a touch of Highland grandeur. The rock is one we have now become familiar with and which we will see again and again before Carlisle is reached. It is the New Red Sandstone, which in the Penrith area is up to 1,000 ft deep.

This tinted rock, which erodes fairly easily, was created over a spell of ninety million years, when this area was an arid desert. Dry easterly winds blew into dunes grains of sand no larger than millet. In course of time these compacted to become sandstone. In the absence of water, highly oxidised iron compounds were to give the rock its reddish-brown coloration.

For the most part, the river Eden is out of sight to rail passengers. In this wooded area a rail passenger might have a fleeting glimpse of a roe or pheasant to hint at the natural bounty. Over the years, a goodly number of pheasants and other game birds must have perished under the wheels of rail traffic.

Those who are stimulated to return to the area by car or on foot will discover that in the vicinity of the Eden Gorge the old-time landowners were an imaginative, even eccentric lot who could not resist tampering with the soft, easily worked sandstone. They blasted recesses to create footways, as at the Nunnery Walks just north of Kirkoswald. Near the village of Little Salkeld, Lt-Col Samuel Lacy arranged for a series of five cavities in the form of rooms to be cut into a cliff high above the river.

Baron Wood Tunnels

This is a grand name for something as prosaic as two short railway tunnels, which are numbered 1 and 2. The first tunnel has a length of 207 yards and was finished with red sandstone side walls, arch and facing. There are patches of brickwork on the arch. Tunnel No.2 is of the same type of construction but sightly longer at 251 yards.

The Midland provided a private siding at Baron Wood for the use of the Ley family of Lazonby Hall, who had extensive forestry interests in the Eden Gorge. During the 1914-18 war, pit props, fashioned at a sawmill, were transported from Baron Wood Sidings, which were closed in 1951.

Armathwaite

Firstly, a 325 yard long tunnel known as Cat Clint. Then a viaduct, for the Settle-Carlisle is still running on a high ledge above the river. The viaduct is of nine spans and has a slight curve, being unusual in these parts because it is formed entirely of stone. There is not a brick to be seen. The railway is borne on slender piers at an elevation of 80 ft.

Armathwaite village, a little distance from the station, has a huge redstone bridge—and quite a number of notices drawing attention to the private nature of the ground beside the river. The stationmaster at Armathwaite bestrode the platform with the assurance of a feudal lord on a castle rampart. He had a relatively large staff to do his bidding. One Stationmaster was always nattering about promotion, so he was given it—from this delectable area of Edenvale to t'Collieries. He did not like the prospect, but had to take what he was offered. Otherwise no other offer would have come his way.

A Blackpool man who obtained a job as a porter at Armathwaite did not stay long, being uneasy in the presence of livestock. He told a colleague about the previous night's main job—handling a wagonload of 'bulls', which were actually cows, adding lamely: "I got shuntin' pole at 'em through t'wagons but I couldn't mak 'em do as I wanted."

Dry Beck Viaduct

This seven-span, 80 ft high structure has a length of 139 yards and was built of stone, with brick arch rings.

Armathwaite Signal Boxes

In the summer of 1992, Friends of the Settle-Carlisle completed their first signal box restoration project, which was at Armathwaite, where the box was of Midland origin, dated 1899, being constructed from prefabricated sections to their standard 'Type 2' design. This box differed from others in its greater height, giving the signalman an unimpeded view of the goods yard when the refuge siding immediately in front of the box was occupied.

The box was closed in 1883 and began to deteriorate, in part through vandalism. In collaboration with British Rail, who carried out the vital corner post repairs, the Friends attended to the woodwork and repainted, using specially mixed colours. The Midland colour scheme was adopted, giving the box a rarity value which is appreciated by knowing rail travellers.

Low House Crossing has a box dating from 1890, the present frame having been brought into use in 1900. Crossing gates were replaced by lifting barriers in 1975. The road crosses the Settle-Carlisle on the skew.

Cotehill Viaduct

A short viaduct of 91 yards, it crosses High Stand Gill. Stone was used for the main work, with brick for the parapet wall and arch rings.

Cumwhinton

The medium-sized station closed in 1956. The signal box was put out of use two years later.

Scotby

A medium size station, and the most northerly of Midland type, Scotby was closed in 1942. Scotby had its moment of excitement prior to 1914 when the Allandale Wolf, a noted sheep worrier, was picked up dead on the track. Sammy

Crunkhorn was examining his length one Sunday when he found the wolf lying dead on the track. A photographer was contacted. He took pictures of the beast which were issued in postcard form.

Carlisle

Now for the clatter of Carlisle. The line passes the site of Durran Hill sidings and engine shed and joins the major Lancaster-Carlisle system at Petteril Bridge Junction.

Carlisle Citadel station has an architectural style known as 'Victorian Tudor'. The Midland were the seventh railway company to use the station, and until the amalgamations of 1923 each company organised its own traffic and maintenance facilities. Coats of arms of some of the companies used to adorn the Stationmaster's Office and are now on display in Tullie House, Carlisle.

The 150th anniversary of the opening of Citadel Station occurs in 1997. The City Council are co-ordinating a year-long celebration, including an exhibition of archival material, guided tours, a commemorative service at the Cathedral, display of steam engines, an exhibition about Cowan Sheldon, 'cranemakers to the world', and a railway gala night.

The oldest railmen remember lodging at Carlisle in conditions which were not quite up to hotel standard. Of the 'barracks' at Upperby, which stood in a loco yard, it was claimed they were so crowded a man had to wait for a bed to be vacated. A guard recalled that "we'd have something to eat, and then the chap in charge would sit and play cards with us. When it came to six o'clock he would say: 'Sorry, lads, but you'll have to make your own beds. I'm going home'."

And so, after a journey on the Settle-Carlisle, must we...

A Personal Record of the Settle-Carlisle Experience

DATE	LOCATION	NOTES

DATE	LOCATION	NOTES

DATE	LOCATION	NOTES

ARTEN GILL VIADUCT FROM THE EAST,
SHOWING THE SPOIL HEAPS BEHIND.